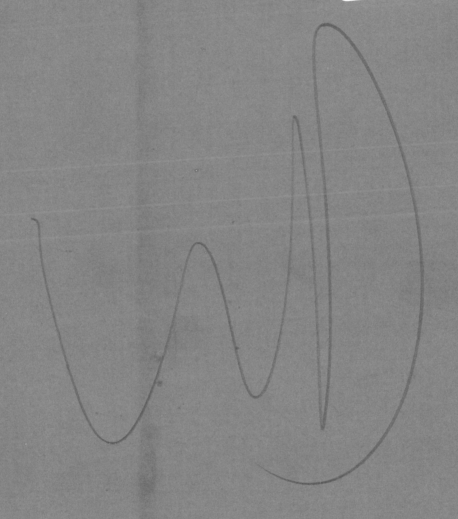

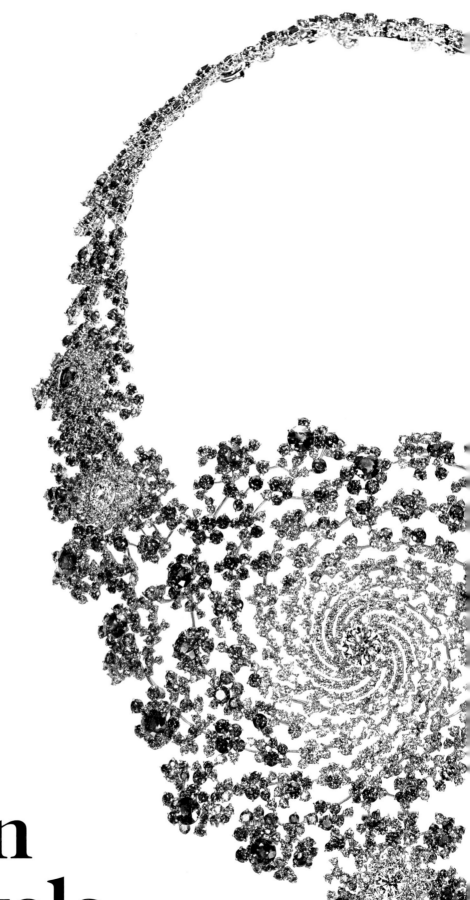

Fashion
for Jewels

Fashion for Jewels

100 Years of Styles and Icons

Carol Woolton

PRESTEL

Munich • Berlin • London • New York

Contents

Introduction

A beautiful jewel is more than just the sum of its parts. Precious metal, stones or shimmering pearls must be combined with the right proportions, use of colour, exquisite workmanship and design. Within this mix the most important ingredient is design — effectively the blueprint of the jewel. In the hands of great designers a piece of jewellery can become a precious, sculpted snapshot, encapsulating the fine and decorative arts, fashion, cinema and architecture of the time it was made, reflecting like a mirror the current zeitgeist and social history of the period.

Originally jewels were a symbol of wealth rather than of style. But over the last hundred years jewellery has become increasingly linked to fashion. During the Belle Époque striking similarities between the ranges of couturiers and jewellers began to emerge. Chiffon and crepe-de-chine corseted dresses were embroidered with silver and gold roses and lilies, the motifs of turn-of-the-century Garland-style jewels. In turn the latter mimicked the net-like fabric techniques of fashion, using gossamer-thin threads of platinum to support dazzling webs of white diamonds and pearls. The formality of the strict Versailles Code, which controlled what was and was not suitable as a motif for formal diamond jewellery, was swept away as jewellery designers began working closely with fashion designers to create a new vocabulary for modern jewels.

Haute joaillerie houses produced their vision for the current look, whether for the Little Black Dresses of the Roaring Twenties, Mary Quant's miniskirts during the 1960s' youth-quake or the candy-floss-coloured silks and satins of spring 2009. With great foresight Louis Cartier saw that haute joaillerie would benefit by joining forces with fashion. In 1898 he moved his Paris premises to Rue de La Paix, a street burgeoning with couturiers such as the House of Worth, hat and glove businesses and perfume manufacturers, and this gave Cartier a creative incentive to make jewellery part of a woman's whole image. At the 1925 Exposition des Arts Décoratifs, from which Art Deco jewels took their name, he did not exhibit Cartier jewels in the Grand Palais with other jewellers, choosing instead the Pavillon de L'Élégance alongside the couturiers.

The strong geometric shapes of a modernist piece by George Fouquet or Jean Després immediately evoke the new Machine Age of the 1930s. The designers' interest in circles, angles and arcs using industrial-style silver cogs and yellow gold ball-bearings, illustrates the precision and robustness of the Jazz Age, and conjures up images of liberated women such as Josephine Baker who pinned the creations to their bold tailored suits.

Coco Chanel was one of the first couturiers to turn her hand to jewellery design creating, with Sicilian nobleman Fulco di Verdura, the iconic bejewelled Maltese Cross cuff which has recently enjoyed a fashion renaissance. Jean Schlumberger worked with Elsa Schiaparelli and Pierre Sterlé collaborated with both Jacques Fath and Christian Dior, bringing to haute joaillerie a sense of stylishness and flamboyance previously only associated with costume jewels. Fashion magazines began to give readers guidance on how to make these modern jewellery designs an integral part of their fashion look. In *Harper's Bazaar* in 1937 Diana Vreeland instructed:

> *'For town this winter: Chanel's waistcoat of black suede with black wool knit sleeves and all your jewels pulled out on top. Jewelry: Wear a blue sapphire thistle in one ear and a ruby thistle in the other. On each lapel pin a larger thistle, the colour reversed.'*

More recently fashion and jewellery have become virtually integrated as major fashion houses such as Chanel, Dior, Gucci, Armani, Versace, Hermès and Louis Vuitton create their own fine jewellery collections to accompany their runway fashion shows. There are many similarities in tradition between the jewellers, who painstakingly transform multi-coloured ribbons of precious stones, gossamer threads of metal and tassels of diamonds into high jewellery creations, and the seamstresses and embroiderers of the couture houses who whip up elaborate frothy extravaganzas from shimmering clouds of tulle and lace. And this was acknowledged in 2010 during Paris Couture Week as the Fédération Française de la Couture included haute joaillerie in its fashion show schedules for the first time.

Vogue wrote in 1939: 'Perhaps too, in these times of uncertainty, the eyes turn to bona fide jewels for their very certainty — for their tangible beauty in a world of all too little beauty, for their tangible value in a world of all too many teetering values'. And still today times may change and fashions come and go but the eternal joy of a jewel resonates through the years.

Elephant ring by Boucheron.

Belle Époque

*'Dressed in black mousseline de soie,
a wide diamond collar supported against
the throat … a collet necklace and a long
chain of diamonds falling over the dress,
and in the coiffure an aigrette of diamonds
with osprey plume and diamond arrow.'*

A 1900 society magazine describes Princess Alexandra at the theatre

The style during the Belle Époque—the beautiful era—was for opulence and extravagance. It was a luxurious lull of peace and sumptuous fashion before the storm and sombre uniforms of World War I. During 1880 in the United States there were few millionaires but by the end of 1890 over one thousand were documented. This new money required status so the Vanderbilts and Astors travelled to Europe searching for marriageable members of the nobility. Paris was the first stop on their stately itinerary to visit the couturiers who had established the city as the epitome of taste. The House of Worth on Rue de La Paix was the most famous salon, conveniently located next door to Cartier, who had moved to the street in 1898. The marriage of Louis Cartier to Andrée Worth the same year strengthened the collaboration between the two houses, creating a homogenous look for their clients' clothes and jewels.

The Edwardian fashion for high collars which elongated the neck, 'S-bend' corsets and lavish hats with plumes of exotic feathers with a fox-fur thrown around the shoulders gave Belle Époque women a swaying grandeur. Belle Époque jewellers were on a parallel grandiloquent path designing jewels set with an array of bows, swags, ribbons and flowers, known as the Versailles Code, considered the only suitable motif for formal diamond jewellery. The lightness of these glittering jewellery pieces chimed with the satins, chiffon and crepe-de-chine fabrics. The inspiration for the Garland style had come from jewels made for Empress Eugénie of France, who had them re-set in the style of Marie Antoinette using the motifs of the 18th century—dainty swags of ribbons and garlands of flowers with elaborate tassels of diamonds. This look is referenced today in Vivienne Westwood's whalebone corsets with nipped-in waists above a bustled behind, or John Galliano's blood-red fitted jackets with peplums over tweed side-saddle hunting skirts.

For Nicole Kidman as courtesan Satine in the 2001 film *Moulin Rouge* jeweller Stefano Canturi recreated a spectacular Garland-style necklace of 1,400 diamonds set into an elaborate collar. Satine was also the inspiration behind the modern *Gaité Parisienne* collection by Boucheron, who created a diamond-set chandelier cage with 899 diamonds hanging with a huge pear-shaped stone.

Top: In Deep Shrimp fleur de lis pendant with black opal by Stephen Webster.
Above: Princess Olga Paley, with her hourglass figure and swags of jewels, exemplified the Belle Époque style.

Platinum and Diamonds

The delicate proportions and awe-inspiring finesse of the Garland style were made possible by two important discoveries at the turn of the 19th century: platinum and the new South African diamonds. Platinum was first discovered by the Spanish in Colombia and named *platina* (small silver). However it was only used in jewellery when a research chemist in 1900 discovered the melting point which made the metal malleable. Superior to silver, which oxidised and tarnished, platinum keeps its reflective matt surface indefinitely, and its blue-grey tinge provides the perfect backdrop to show off the brilliance of white diamonds. A strong metal, it could be used in thinner quantities than gold or silver, making the delicate work of fringing, intricate scrolls and millegrain setting (tiny platinum bead work) possible in elaborate Belle Époque diamond collars. The major diamond sources in India and Brazil had run dry by the late 19th century, and so a shepherd boy stumbling across a large shiny pebble near Kimberley—the 83.5-carat Star of South Africa—heralded the diamond rush. The boy swapped the stone for a horse, ten oxen, and 500 sheep. It was later sold to the Countess of Dudley for £25,000. A farm sold for prospecting for £6,300 by two brothers called De Beers in the 1870s has produced £600 million worth of gems over 100 years.

Below left: Bow-knot brooch by Cartier Paris, 1907. Platinum, round old- and rose-cut diamonds.
Below right: Lily stomacher brooch by Cartier Paris, 1906. Platinum, round old- and rose-cut diamonds, millegrain setting.
Bottom left: Scroll tiara by Cartier Paris, 1910. Platinum and diamonds, millegrain setting.

Queen Alexandra (1844–1925)

With coronation celebrations that lasted a year in 1902 King Edward VII and Queen Alexandra were the templates for Belle Époque high living. After the heavy Gothic-style fashion for black mourning jewellery which had dominated Queen Victoria's reign the world was ready to be captivated by Alexandra's style for bejewelled Edwardian elegance. Her deceptively simple shimmering lavender and pastel-coloured gowns by British dressmaker Redfern (who also made for Queen Victoria and Lillie Langtry) were covered with high-necked diamond and pearl chokers (worn to hide a scar on her neck) and a bodice plastered in delicate diamond brooches and royal diamond orders topped off with her dashing Russian fringe tiara. Alexandra was an early trendsetter in the art of layering, wearing many strands of pearl necklaces long and low as sautoirs. In 1904 Cartier made her quintessential Belle Époque necklace set with Indian rubies, emeralds and diamonds which were mounted on fine gossamer threads suspended from a choker and hanging across the throat supporting leafy garlands and diamond bows. Combining fashion and jewellery designers began stitching platinum and diamond scrolls and garlands onto black ribbons to tie around the neck, following Alexandra, and Edgar Degas painted his ballet dancers wearing similar black velvet ribbons.

Top left: Loie necklace by Boucheron.
Top right: Satine necklace by Boucheron.
Above: François Flameng, Queen Alexandra, 1908.

'Fleur, faune and femme.'
René Lalique

Art Nouveau

A feminine decorative art form which ended the 19th century, Art Nouveau had a great impact on jewellery. It still resonates today in artists' jewellery where gemstones do not dominate the design of a piece. The movement began in the workshops and galleries of the art world. Its leaders were John Ruskin and William Morris, and it rapidly became one of the first 'lifestyle' trends, influencing interiors, architecture and furniture design as well as jewellery and fashion. More than a style it was a way of thinking which broke the connections with classical styles and made even the most functional object a work of art, for example Hector Guimard's entrances to the Paris Métro, made in metal and glass as urban art for the masses. It was an apposite trend for the increasing number of unmarried working women in shops and offices for whom fashion and jewels had hitherto been elitist.

The name came from La Maison de l'Art Nouveau, a shop opened in Paris in 1895 by Siegfried Bing, and it caught on as a generic term to describe a look characterised by sinuous curves and inspiration from nature. Orchids, which could now be grown under glass thanks to cheap coal and labour, became a powerful symbol of the movement. Advertising posters, accepted as art for the first time, showed romanticized images of women with long flowing strands of golden hair and free-flowing lines with an almost supernatural feel. Leg-of-mutton sleeves and skirts flounced out like elegant trumpets of a blossoming flower with graceful embellishments such as flowing embroidery borders echoed the forms of stylised jewelled flowers. These long-limbed beauties often turned into a winged bird or a flower. In turn the dragonfly jewels were depicted as half-woman and half-insect, and nude female figures in moulded glass jewels metamorphosed into extraordinary creatures with butterfly wings — all references to the oncoming emancipation of women. So many high floral fashions in the Art Nouveau style were made for the London department store Liberty that the Italians came to call the movement *Stile Liberty*.

Top: Brooch by Lalique, c. 1897–98. Chased gold, enamel, brilliants, baroque pearl, pendant.
Centre: Brooch by Moira Fine Jewellery.
Above: Gustav Klimt, Judith and the Head of Holofernes, 1901.

Sarah Bernhardt (1844–1923)

Women were represented in Art Nouveau in every medium from metalwork to architecture, prints and paintings. But the most famous of these was the celebrated French stage actress of the 19th century, the 'Divine' Sarah Bernhardt. Just as today celebrity is used as a 'face' to represent the values of a particular brand, La Bernhardt literally became the poster girl for the Art Nouveau movement. The revolutionary poster designed by Alphonse Mucha for Bernhardt's 1894 play *Gismonda* resulted in instant fame and many commissions for the artist. The poster was typical of Mucha's style, showing Bernhardt as a healthy young woman in flowing neo-classical robes, printed with organic patterns and vine-like tresses, surrounded by lush flowers like a halo behind her head. Mucha also forged a commercial alliance with Bernhardt, designing all her posters, costumes, sets and personal knickknacks such as a serpent-shaped ring and bracelet realised by jeweller George Fouquet.

René Lalique (1860–1945)

René Lalique, who had founded the eponymous brand in 1885, designed Bernhardt's flamboyant and melodramatic stage jewellery. His Art Nouveau style is credited with transforming French jewellery from an industry into an art. He relegated diamonds and precious stones to a secondary role, making the design of a piece of jewellery paramount, and preferring to work with new valueless materials such as horn, ivory and glass set into fine gold with matching tones in shimmery enamel. In his hands hard, brittle stones became the gossamer wings of a dragonfly, fragile enamel maple leaves or the soft petals of a poppy. His use of flowers was supremely democratic, using exotic blossom-laden Japanese cherries, sycamore seed pods and pansies, but also embracing the humble thistle and dandelion. He reflected the quiet drama of the change of seasons, from a young bud to a flower disintegrating in the wind or dying with wilting petals. Echoing the fashions Lalique's female forms in moulded or frosted glass were sensual Bernhardt-like nymphs or sylphs. He twisted them into the fluid lines of Art Nouveau with floaty fabrics draped around their rippling hair and wrapped in flowers as symbols of the seasons. Often two women were shown together, symbolising female harmony at the end of a male-dominated century.

Today the furnaces at Lalique are still blasting, the glass is collected by Sir Elton John and Stella McCartney, and the *Cabochon* ring, designed by René Lalique, made in fourteen shades of glass, is still their bestseller. Lalique's original themes of *fleur*, *faune* and *femme* are kept alive with a trendy twist and forward-looking feel.

Above: Brooch by Boucheron, 1907.
Below left: Neck pendant/brooch, Winged Woman, by Lalique c. 1897–99. Gold, enamel, diamonds.
Below right: Fleur d'Éclat necklace by Lalique, 2010.

Dark Designs

In modern times the dark glamour of the Goth style originated in the 1980s in a London nightclub called The Batcave, primarily as a backlash against the colourful disco fashion of the 1970s. The early style icons of the movement were bands such as The Cure and Siouxsie & the Banshees, whose music celebrated the dark, shadowy side of life and a fascination with death. The Goths drew inspiration from Victorian writers such as Edgar Allan Poe and Bram Stoker who combined romance and horror to conjure the ultimate Goth fashion icon — the vampire. The success of recent screen sensations *Twilight* and *True Blood* has made vampire chic fashionable once again — a look which requires dark and melancholic crushed-velvet skirts overlaid with lace, Victorian-style tail-coats and ruffled Regency-style shirts.

In 2008, Giles Deacon sent his models down the runway with their heads wrapped in black veils which he described as 'femme fatales in a gothic disco'. Although the look has an androgynous appeal, Goth girls keep their femininity with tight bodices that draw attention to nipped-in waists. Corsets have sweetheart necklines or intricate satin panels and tailored jackets are laced up with satin ribbons pulled tight through silver hoops. A sombre tulip-shaped skirt with layers of lace trim will be accessorised with spiked wristbands or studded leather gloves. There has been a 'haute Goth' fashion trend in recent shows by John Galliano for Christian Dior, Rick Owens and Ann Demeulemeester. Alexander McQueen's models wearing cinched-in corsetry and eyes rimmed with kohl stalk the runways, redolent of high Victoriana, wearing raven feathers, fishnets, close-fitting riding jackets and spike-heeled boots. Goth sensibilities love religious iconography: Tilda Swinton wore blood-red taffeta by John Galliano hung with a huge crucifix; and Riccardo Tisci at Givenchy burnt large crucifixes onto cobwebby black knits with crosses on heavy gold chains. Queen of the Vamps is the young Angelina Jolie (her teenage ambition was to become a funeral director), and she still attends Academy Awards ceremonies wearing Morticia Addams-style long, clinging black dresses, her pallid complexion framed in long, black straight hair. She famously married her first husband, actor Jonny Lee Miller, wearing leather trousers and a white shirt with his name splashed in her blood.

Top: Raven skull ring in silver with enamel by Philippa Holland.
Centre: Flying Fish brooch from Fly By Night collection by Stephen Webster. 18ct white gold, diamonds, black sapphires, and green tourmalines.
Above: Russell Brand wearing typically Goth jewellery.

Above: Stephen Webster.
Below left: Beetle
by Stephen Webster.
Below right: Dragonfly
by Stephen Webster.
Bottom left: Rosehip bracelet
by Stephen Webster.
Bottom right: Black-and-white gold
Dragonfly brooch with micro-pavé-set
black and white round diamonds, flat
diamond wings, and tiger's-eye eyes
by Jacob & Co.

Stephen Webster (1959–)

The ornate filigree metalwork of jeweller Stephen Webster draws inspiration from
the Gothic or blackletter style of calligraphy and printing, with its dark, angular
and complex fonts. Obsessed by the age of Charles Dickens, Webster himself sports
a glamorous Goth style, wearing black leather with intricate silver necklaces and
black diamonds glinting at his earlobes above his high-necked collars. He works with
blackened silver and gold, giving his pieces a light, feminine feel despite the underlying
dark themes of collections such as *Blade* which has knife-like edges in diamonds and
green tsavorites. Pretty wild-rose cuffs in rose-cut diamonds with rose quartz alongside
shimmering black moonstones and graduated pink sapphires have finger-pricking thorns
on spiky stems. Webster's motifs include nocturnal creatures such as bats, griffins,
stag beetles and moths which he lends jewelled bodies and delicate diamond-set wings.
Like shards of shattered glass he uses black mother-of-pearl and hematite and blue gold
stone in his silver collection, which draws inspiration from the beautiful stained-glass
windows under the high vaulted arches of Gothic cathedrals.

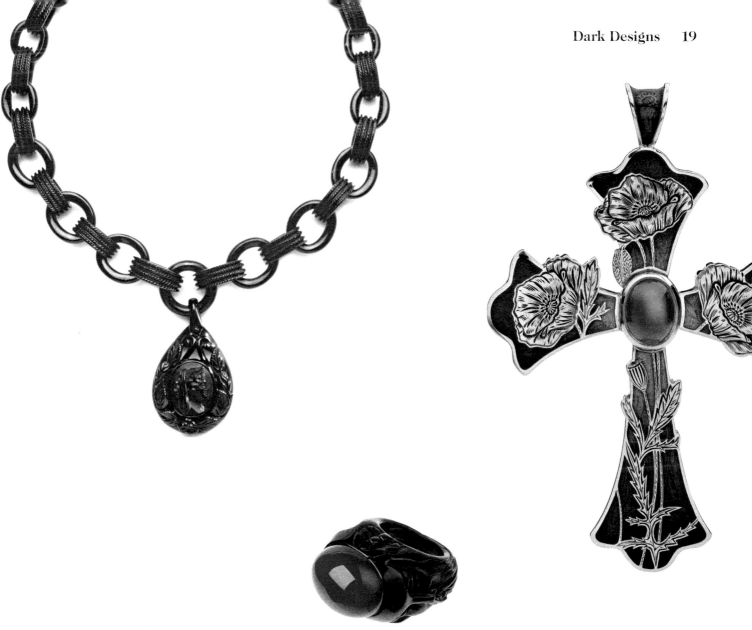

Dark Jewels

Victorian mourning jewels, made fashionable in the 19th century by Queen Victoria following the death of Prince Albert, make the ideal fashion statement for Goths as they are associated with death and are literally jet black. Made from Whitby jet, a fossilized coal, the translucent stone was sculpted into lacy chokers and dark cameo brooches for women to coordinate with their mourning black clothes. The Victorian trend of wearing a lock of a lost loved-one's hair, designed into a ring or locket, is a macabre fashion forerunner of Angelina Jolie and second husband Billy Bob Thornton's fascination for wearing vials of each other's blood, hanging like brilliant crimson pendants around their necks. For modern, anti-establishment Goths the religious symbolism of crucifixes, rosary beads and ankhs (the Egyptian symbol for eternal life) becomes purely decorative. Jeweller Theo Fennell hand-crafts black enamel with engraved rose gold to give a *trompe-l'oeil* effect to Gothic-style crosses, and sets showy tombstone styles with black and white diamonds. In tune with McQueen's black corseted tulle fairy dresses he creates precious devils and fairies as well as golden dragons, griffins and rising phoenixes that you might find in a fairy tale by the Brothers Grimm.

Top left: Necklace from an English parure set in jet, late 19th century.
Centre: Molten onyx ring with red carnelian by Muriel Grateau.
Top right: 18ct rose gold, ruby cabochon, hand-engraved and black-enamelled poppy cross by Theo Fennell.
Above: Fire of London bracelet by Stephen Webster.

Art Deco

'Chanel originated the absolutely simple frock, a mode that demands jewels to save it from being drab.'

Vogue, 1926

The years following World War I saw the emergence of a new type of woman. So it was with great foresight that Louis Cartier, on a menu at the Paris Ritz, jotted down the first sketches of Art Deco jewellery to suit these women's dynamic, emanicipated lifestyle. Echoing the new style of architecture based on geometric shapes, these sketches showed simple cubes, polygons and rhombuses in unusual colour combinations. Diamonds were the foundation of this new style: circular brilliants sparkled alongside square and emerald cuts and the new baguette cut (named after the French loaf) appeared. Together they created a pavéd effect of diamond step patterns and heavy semi-circular links, mimicking the facades of modern skyscrapers. Deco girls swung with long pendant-style earrings, often reaching as low as the shoulder. They wore waist-length necklaces with diamond-set tassels, or pendants worn with fur-trimmed capes shimmering with golden braid and fringes. Sleeveless dresses made diamond bracelets the new must-have for bare wrists and upper arms. The term Deco was abbreviated from the Exposition Internationale des Arts Décoratifs held in Paris in 1925 where Cartier was the only jeweller who did not exhibit in the Grand Palais, opting instead to show his designs on mannequins alongside fashion houses such as Chanel and Paul Poiret.

The Art Deco skyline of New York continues to inspire Harry Winston who produces baguette-cut pendants in the shape of the Empire State Building and cabochon sapphire *Skyscraper* rings. Nearly 70 years after the opening of the Empire State Building designer Holly Fulton was inspired to produce a collection described as 'Art Deco gone pop'. Graphic tangerine and blue felt wool dresses decorated with perspex and crystals in large triangular and rectangular shapes like ultra-modern flapper girls swung down the runway with huge skyscraper crystal bangles and earrings. Jessica McCormack creates *New New York* diamond *Skyscape* rings and Matina Amanita makes miniature Chrysler Buildings for fingers.

Top left: Coral and black enamel necklace by Jean Fouquet, 1929.
Top right: Egyptian-style pendant by Cartier Paris, 1913. Platinum; old-, single- and rose-cut diamonds in round, triangular and pear-shaped forms; calibré-cut and fancy-cut onyx gemstones; millegrain setting.
Above: Manhattan ring by Matina Amanita; Skyscraper ring by Harry Winston.

Jeanne Boivin (1959–)

The sister of couturier Paul Poiret, Jeanne Boivin grew up immersed in artistic
and fashionable worlds which influenced her revolutionary style of jewels. She ignored
the prevailing fashion for diamond strap bracelets, creating instead voluptuous feminine
shapes such as a gold and twisted silver 'barbaric' rope bangle. With a look that
encompassed the geometric and abstract as well as the naturalistic she used simple
but original ideas and concepts. Slicing into a melon one day at breakfast, she was
inspired by the melon seeds to create a platinum curved bangle with a central
diamond shape filled with diamond 'seeds'. She took the fashion for colour beyond
the Deco palette of coral, emerald and onyx, using large semi-precious stones such
as aquamarines, citrines and amethysts, and was the first jeweller to combine
sandalwood and ebony with gold.

Vanity Cases

By 1921 fifty million women were wearing lipstick and cosmetics had become big business. Fashionable women now had to carry around make-up as well as cigarettes and other items. But how? Charles Arpels, co-founder of Van Cleef & Arpels, watched in horror one day as Florence Jay Gould, the wife of a railroad magnate, tossed the things she needed for an evening out into a simple metal box. In response Arpels created the elegant Minaudière in yellow gold and lacquer with gem-set motifs and diamond clasps. 'Arranged as a miniscule closet' according to a contemporary advertisement, the Minaudière opens to reveal a range of golden accessories such as a powder compact, folding opera-glasses, a lighter, lipstick holder, cigarette case, retractable watch and tortoise-shell comb, as well as a mirror on the inside lid.

Above. Vanity cases by Van Cleef & Arpels and Boucheron (bottom right).

'Today's pearls aren't the sort your Sloaney aunt would wear with her twinset: they've come over all casual.'

Cressida Connolly

Twinset and Pearls

Twinsets first appeared in the 1940s as the archetypal look of young English roses for whom a warm wool jumper and matching cardigan provided a cosy chic look for their country life. Popular from the Shires to Sloane Square, the tight-fitting jumper and unbuttoned cardigan was worn with a girl's first piece of jewellery — often a strand of pearls inherited from a doting grandmother. Historically pearls are a symbol of purity and have always been considered the most appropriate jewel for young unmarried women as well as a basic staple of the jewellery box. The conservative *Country Life* magazine frontispiece photograph of a well-bred and well-groomed debutante, often announcing her engagement, became known as 'girls with pearls' and defined the look as classic fashion.

Sex goddesses of the 1950s such as Jayne Mansfield and Diana Dors borrowed the look ironically, stretching tiny sweaters to emphasise their generous embonpoints when they wanted to do 'demure'. Gradually 'twinset and pearls' became a reference for old-fashioned and frumpy. But now there is the modernist twinset brigade let by Pringle, famous for their safe Scottish woollens, who dusted off their traditional image in 2002, showing their models naked except for glistening strands of pearls. Fashion designers such as Alexander McQueen and Michael Kors have used the twinset-and-pearls reference as a fast-track way of creating a polished lady-like look, accessorising classics like textured tweed suits and languid silk blouses with elegant strings of white pearls.

Top left and right: Pearl ring and earrings by Mikimoto.
Above: Pearl necklace by Delfina Delettrez.

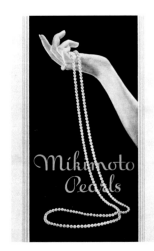

Top left: Necklace from Midnight
collection by Mikimoto.
Centre: Yagurama sash clip
by Mikimoto.
Above: Vintage Mikimoto
advertisement.
Centre pages: Pearl necklace
by Cassandra Goad.

Kokichi Mikimoto (1858–1954)

During the 19th century pearl beds were fished virtually to the point of extinction, and pearls would have disappeared from fashion altogether had it not been for Japanese pearl farmer Kokichi Mikimoto's determination to produce the world's first 'cultured' spherical pearl. As protection, an oyster covers anything entering its shell with layers of thin mother-of-pearl (nacre), effectively turning the intruder into a magical, gleaming pearl. Mikimoto perfected the art of 'culturing' pearls, introducing tiny beads into the oyster in controlled conditions, and protecting the animals for a couple of years before harvesting the gems. At the start in 1905, the cultured oysters were lowered in bamboo baskets back into the sea. But today Mikimoto is a highly scientific industry, even monitoring the breath of the oyster to protect them from choking to death in polluted seas, with the aim of preventing a pearl shortage similar to the turn of the last century. Working with Mikimoto, couturier Yohji Yamamoto has created the *Stormy Weather* collection of black-and-white pearls, designs which perfectly complement his simple Japanese-style silhouettes. Other famous pearl fans include Marilyn Monroe who was given a strand of Mikimoto pearls on her honeymoon by husband Joe DiMaggio, and Sarah Jessica Parker who sparked a rush for long, swinging 32-inch opera-length strands as Carrie Bradshaw in the movie *Sex and the City*.

Diana, Princess of Wales (1961–97)

From the moment she appeared in the public eye Diana, Princess of Wales embraced the pearl choker as her jewel of choice almost as much as Princess Alexandra had done 80 years earlier. In her formal engagement photographs with the Queen the shy, young Diana Spencer appeared wearing a simple sailor suit and string of pearls. In the context of marriage pearls are used to symbolise a wife's chastity, so ten thousand pearls decorated the 25-foot train of Diana's ivory silk wedding gown made by David and Elizabeth Emanuel. The pearl choker with a large teardrop pendant worn to the wedding ceremony by Diana's sister, Lady Sarah McCorquodale, was quickly swapped onto the neck of the new Princess of Wales after the reception above the coral-coloured bolero jacket of her going-away outfit. When the newlyweds docked at Gibraltar during the honeymoon another pearl choker with a turquoise flower made an appearance, worn with a red, blue and white flowered silk dress. The innocence of the pearl suited the blushing Diana in the early years of her marriage and complemented her youthful style of white pie-frill collars and fairytale frothy pastel-coloured Bellville Sassoon evening gowns with satin bows, ribbons and sashes.

Top left: Mouchette earrings by Belmacz.
Top right: South Sea pearl necklace by Autore.
Above: *Princess Diana, 1984.*

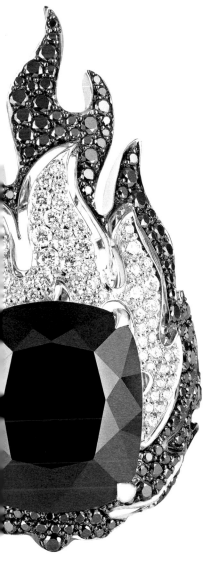

Magnificent Monochrome

'I said that black had everything. White too. They have an absolute beauty. It's the perfect match.'

Coco Chanel

Since the 1920s the modest monochrome of black and white has been a classic combination in art, architecture and the salons of fashion designers. Like yin and yang, opposites attracting to make a perfect match, monochrome's clean lines are given a fresh twist each season. Coco Chanel created the Little Black Dress which she brought to life with stark snow-white fluted collars, opalescent frosted camellia petals or chalky-white strands of pearls. Today Karl Lagerfeld, sporting his own monochrome style of white high-necked dress shirts worn with black leather, reinterprets black-and-white themes for the Chanel runway each season. Lagerfeld not only juxtaposes the colours but also plays with contrasting fabrics, mixing heavy black velvets and flecked tweeds with light icy-white crochet and lace. A white tweed wool suit is trimmed with black-and-white braid and a black satin belt embellished with black jet and pearls. Iridescent black chiffon is frosted with camellia-white cuffs, trimmed with a bouquet of white satin flowers and pinned with a black or white diamond camellia brooch.

    In recent years Riccardo Tisci at Givenchy has shown sharply tailored black-and-white chiffon robes with gilded embroidery, inspired by medieval queens. Gareth Pugh creates beautiful black-and-white chequered cashmere dresses creating an optical illusion as they undulate around the body. Moschino, Armani, Louis Vuitton and Alexander McQueen have all given 19th-century black-and-white hound's tooth and salt-and-pepper tweeds a 21st-century makeover. The wool creates a slick urban silhouette suited to sophisticated city living rather than the country life for which the fabrics were first manufactured. Bright luminescent pearls lend light relief to 'dark' looks, while menacing inky-coloured black diamonds and pearls give a contemporary visual impact to classic white.

Top left: Flame ring with garnet, Fire of London collection by Stephen Webster for Garrard.
Top right: Hypnôse bracelet, white gold with a blackened finish and diamonds by Cartier.
Above: Chanel prêt-à-porter, spring/ summer 2007.

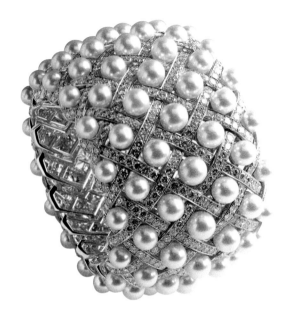

Gabrielle Chanel (1883–1971)

One of the most stylish women of the 20th century Gabrielle 'Coco' Chanel's creativity acted as a catalyst for change in the fashion world. Inspired by the wardrobes of her wealthy male lovers she created a new spirit in dressing for modern independent women with her sporty jersey dresses, slim lines, bobbed hair, red lipstick and trousers. 'In a black pullover and ten ropes of white pearls she revolutionised fashion', said Christian Dior. She was the first advocate of mixing *faux* with fine jewels, often riding through the park with her lover, the Duke of Westminster, while wearing her own magnificent oriental pearls among strings of fakes. During a diamond slump in the 1930s Gabrielle was approached by the Union of Diamond Merchants to boost sales with a new jewellery collection. In 1932 she created dazzling celestial comets and stars with ribbon-like bows, braids and fringes in glacial white platinum and diamonds as the perfect accompaniment to her Little Black Dress.

Chanel today has breathed new life into the monochrome trend with black-and-white enamel cuffs embellished with a crystal double 'C' and Maltese Cross, two-tone pumps and quilted bags with gilt chains, white lambskin gloves with glazed leather straps and black-and-white ceramic *J12* watches. Bejewelled camellias twinkle with thousands of black-and-white diamonds, and fine jewellery collections with South Sea pearls, brilliant diamonds and sapphires.

Top left: Matelassé Perles bracelet in 18ct yellow gold, set with diamonds for a total weight of 52ct and 105 cultured pearls by Chanel Fine Jewellery.
Top right: Comète necklace in platinum and diamonds created by Mle Chanel in 1932 and redesigned in 1993 for the launch of Chanel Fine Jewellery.
Above: Gabrielle Chanel, 1936.

Black Diamonds

The fashion for black diamonds towards the end of the last century is attributed to Fawaz Gruosi of De Grisogono who boldly designed a ring with a large white pearl set among a mass of inky coloured shimmering black gemstones. A black diamond's dark appearance results from a myriad of microscopic inclusions so unlike white diamonds that they reflect virtually no light internally. Discovered as a by-product of mining for white diamonds, these black stones were traditionally considered valueless and were discarded until Gruosi transformed their tarnished image. He plays with the colour contrast to create black diamond ear clips with a white centre, reversing the colour combination for the other ear; or white pavé-set pagoda-shaped layers of white diamonds holding a perfect black Tahitian pearl drop, with a South Sea drop and black stones completing the pair. White diamonds have a regal brilliance, but when combined with edgy dark stones, they shine with a subtle lustre more in tune with contemporary fashion.

Above: Stingray ring by De Grisogono.
Below left: Spirit of De Grisogono ring.
Below right: Pearl and black diamond earrings by De Grisogono.
Bottom right: Stingray choker by De Grisogono.

The Cocktail Hour

'Cocktail jewellery is about martinis, furs, fast cars and Monte Carlo.'

Geoffrey Munn

Fashionistas in the 1940s had much to overcome with a worldwide cloth shortage and a strict coupon system. With uniforms a part of everyday life, fashion entered a period of restrained sophistication. Sombre, tailored pencil skirts and padded shoulders emphasised feminine strength as women took on the roles of men who were away at war. Their make-do-and-mend style was softened with elaborate curls piled on top of the head, bright lipstick and large precious brooches pinned to lapels to balance square shoulders. Platinum and gold were in short supply so jewellers made deceptively bulky but glamorous pieces, which actually required very little metal. Jewellery design using golden interlaced scrolls, curls, bows and ribbons echoed the draping and pleating of dresses worn at the new 'cocktail parties'. Twinkling around wrists were the new Van Cleef & Arpels *Manhattan* cocktail bracelets, hung with a glass, an ice-pick, a strip of lemon and three tiny golden vermouth, whisky and angostura bitters bottles. The diamond shortage led to the use, in showy 'cocktail' rings, of large square-cut semi-precious stones such as citrines and aquamarines which were easier to acquire from Brazil.

Pierre Balmain's original vision of women in tailored suits has been re-interpreted by the company's present creative director, Christophe Decarnin. For power-dressing in the modern recession Decarnin engineers sharply angled shoulders to draw attention to tiny waists. Over at Lanvin Alber Elbaz gives his suits a 1940s-style exaggerated waist-to-hip ratio by padding the hips of knee-length skirts. Softly sensual Katharine Hepburn look-a-likes sashay down the runways at Dior and Donna Karan, imitating early Hollywood-style fluid-draped silk evening gowns. For party girls sipping the fashionable drink of the new century — the Cosmopolitan — Garrard introduced contemporary cocktail rings with citrines, orange sapphires and garnets on a trellis-work of red and black spinels.

Top: Manhattan cocktail bracelet by Van Cleef & Arpels.
Above: Daisy cocktail ring with blue topaz by Asprey.
Below: Camelot ring with pink opal by Asprey.

Joan Crawford (1905–77)

'The Crawford Look', which epitomised the 1940s' style, was sparked by Joan's 1945 Oscar-winning role in *Mildred Pierce*. Crawford played the role of a housewife who works her way up to become a powerful businesswoman, wearing tailored pinstripe suits with padded shoulders and plain white shirts. The MGM publicity machine ensured there were copies of Joan's movie wardrobes in the stores to coincide with the release of her films. This public look also became Crawford's private style, as she often bought her on-screen gowns to wear off-set because she wanted to 'look every inch a movie star' whenever she appeared in public. As there was no 'loaning' of jewels to movie stars in those days, Crawford amassed a fabulous personal collection which often appeared in her films. Paul Flato's jewellery store on Sunset Boulevard was her regular haunt. There she bought three ruby-and-diamond foliate clips which she used to secure her fashionable turbans. From Raymond C. Yard she acquired sophisticated parures in yellow gold, scroll-design set with large square-cut citrines to clip to the neck of a cocktail dress.

Above: Joan Crawford wearing Verdura, c. 1944.
Below left: Diamond and emerald watch-brooch by Paul Flato, c. 1930.
Below right: 18ct gold, moonstone, sapphire and diamond brooch by Yard, c. 1945.
Bottom left: 14ct rose and yellow gold oak leaf brooch by Yard.
Bottom right: 18ct gold cuff bangle set with rubies and diamonds by Boucheron, c. 1940.

Fulco di Verdura (1898–1978)

The Duke of Verdura (Fulco to his friends) encapsulated the 1940s' style of glamour with his whimsical designs full of vibrant stones. Originally a textile designer for Coco Chanel (who set him the task of re-vamping her jewels) Verdura (with Coco) created the iconic oversized enamel Maltese Cross cuff in 1937. Verdura was considered radical for his use of yellow gold (previously viewed as too casual and sporty for formal fine jewellery) which he wove and twisted into precious, nautical-looking knots. Inspired by the brilliant colours in the garden of his childhood home in Sicily, Verdura created shell brooches encrusted with citrines, sumptuous ruby and peridot pomegranates and golden-linked bracelets, as worn by Greta Garbo. A three-piece ruby-and-diamond brooch worn by Joan Crawford was modelled after parts of the rococo cornice from the ceilings of his family palazzo. Tyrone Power visited Verdura for a gift for his wife and was asked what he wanted to give her. 'If I could', replied the dashing actor, 'I'd give her my heart wrapped up'. In response Verdura designed a ruby cabochon brooch in the shape of heart, tied with a softly knitted gold sash.

Top left: Maltese Cross bracelet with amethyst and peridot by Verdura.
Top right: Wrapped heart brooch with rubies by Verdura.
Centre left: Shell brooch by Verdura.
Centre right: Pomegranate brooch by Verdura.
Above: Coco Chanel and Fulco di Verdura, 1937.

Gilded Geometries

'A wholly modern discipline, based on precision, robustness and the rejection of anything useless or complicated.'

Jean Després

The aesthetic of graphic styles, horizontal lines, and geometric shapes has been a fashion regular since the 1960s. French designer Pierre Cardin gave geometry lessons on crisp, supple textiles featuring circular and rectangular motifs, which became his signature style. The Mod look of dresses in stripes and bold checks worn with 'wet-look' white lace-up boots filled boutiques on London's Carnaby Street and the Kings Road. The cashmere company Pringle have given their argyle diamond-shaped pattern a fashion-forward energy, referencing it with youth sub-cultures in edgy images of Tilda Swinton. Osman Yousefzada explores geometry sending models down the runway wearing all-white dresses with gold embroidered patch pockets and oblong shapes in layered panels of gold. He has pursued the look with a range of symmetrical square-cut rock crystal and sapphire bib-style necklaces and earrings. Geometric jewels and fashion evolved as a desire for something modern, influenced by the architectural Bauhaus movement, searching to define forms in a minimal way. The square and circular onyx and gold shapes of *Bauhaus Multiple* by Julia Muggenburg encapsulates the philosophy in a small piece of jewellery, as well as her *Triangular* rope in gold, onyx and white pearl wheel-shaped *Spitfire* earrings. The *Idole* heavy gold linked bracelets by Hermès echo the work of the early modernists in their classic perfection of circles, angles and arcs.

Top left: Cuff by Ritz Fine Jewellery.
Top right: L'Âme du Voyage necklace by Louis Vuitton.
Above: Bauhaus Multiple in coral and lapis and Spitfire earrings by Julia Muggenburg for Belmacz.

Above: Mary Quant, 1963.
Below left: Idole des Fleurs bracelet by Hermès.
Below right: Bracelet by Hermès.
Bottom left: Farout necklace by Solange Azagury-Partridge.
Bottom right: Cufflinks by Suzanne Syz.

Mary Quant (1934–)

Mary Quant revolutionised fashion with fresh innovative looks that responded to the fast pace of social change in the Swinging Sixties. She drew on geometric shapes for a youthful new look, from her trademark five-point bob haircut by Vidal Sassoon, to her sleek, unstructured clothes. In 1965 she developed the short skirt, 16 centimetres above the knee, which was named after her favourite make of car, the Mini, and worn with patterned tights and vinyl 'go-go' boots. 'Snobbery has gone out of fashion', she declared opening her boutique, Bazaar, which sold the Chelsea Look to liberated working women. She made use of new technology, creating fabrics using PVC, Nylon and Lycra, mixed to be non-crease in her skinny stretch sweaters. Quant was also at the forefront of changes in fashion photography, using wide-eyed, pale-faced models such as Jean Shrimpton, Jan de Villeneuve and Twiggy in child-like poses far removed from the grown-up chic of French haute couture models.

Jean Després (1889–1980)

Collected during his lifetime by Andy Warhol, Jean Després was a French designer and jeweller of the Machine Age, who used uncompromisingly modern geometric motifs in his work following World War I. During the war he had worked on aeroplane design, and this was reflected later in his strong masculine pieces which were snapped up by the liberated women of the Jazz Age such as Josephine Baker. The lines, themes and materials used by Després in his jewels drew inspiration from contemporary life, featuring cranks, blades, gears and pistons. A large brooch would have large silver 'cogs' set among ball-bearings and lined in yellow gold. His flat silver rectangular rings were welded with motifs in red and black enamel or lacquer. Precious but brutal-looking Després' pieces blended well with the energetic casual appeal of the new tailored suits for the modern woman.

Top left: Silver-set chrysophrase and onyx pendant by Després, 1931.
Top right and centre: Valence Plus and Valence collections by Cora Sheibani.
Above: White and yellow gold ring with a citrine by Després.

*'I try to make everything look
as if it were growing uneven,
at random, organic, in motion.'*

Jean Schlumberger at Tiffany

Fashionable Flowers

Floral fabrics are a hardy perennial in fashion, loved for their colourful feminine effect.
But when floral-printed cottons first reached England from Calicut in India (the origin
of the term calico) in the late 17th century, they encountered vigorous campaigns against
such imports by the English woollen industry. In 1720 Parliament enacted a law that
forbade 'the Use and Warings in Apparel of imported chintz, and also its use or Wear
in or about any Bed, Chair, Cushion or other Household furniture'. Women seen
wearing the new fabrics had to run the gauntlet of the anti-calico movement, who would
subject floral-sprigged ladies to violent attacks, even tearing the clothes from their backs.
Newspaper columns targeted women calico consumers, calling them 'jilts', 'satyrs' and
'patched, painted, powder'd Drury Whores'.

Since then many different species of flowers have been used by designers both
as a metaphor for a woman and as a motif to express the zeitgeist of a new generation.
In 1875 Arthur Lasenby Liberty created lavender-sprigged fabrics (called Tana Lawn
after Lake Tana in Ethiopia from where the cotton originated) to appeal to women of all
social classes. And today Liberty still produces classic designs such as William Morris's
bucolic fantasy *Strawberry Thief* alongside new designs by Turner Prize-winning
artist Grayson Perry, who subverts the innocent Liberty depiction of nature for an
environmentally aware new generation. During the 1950s cerise roses were embroidered
on romantic prom-style organza skirts, echoing the voluptuous shapes of a tulip or
bluebell flower. For Mary Quant the daisy expressed the optimistic youth-quake of
the 1960s, and this simple shape adorned her highly modernist make-up, lingerie and
patterned tights. Today designers such as Erdem and Dolce & Gabbana make floral
looks from traditional herbaceous border blooms for retro-romantic styles. Others such
as Matthew Williamson, Stella McCartney and Gucci move towards modern psychedelic
swirling flowers and pixellated patterned hothouse varieties with acid-coloured palettes
which have a computer-generated quality.

Top left: Floral brooch by Adler.
Top right: Floral brooch
by Glenn Spiro.

Top left: Diamond brooch, mounted by Schlumberger.
Top right: Diamond Fleurage necklace set in 18ct gold and platinum by Schlumberger for Tiffany & Co.
Centre left: Citrine and diamond brooch by Schlumberger for Tiffany & Co.
Centre right: 18ct gold, sapphire and emerald brooch by Schlumberger for Tiffany & Co.
Above: Enamelled orchid brooch with diamonds by Tiffany & Co.

Jean Schlumberger (1907–87)

Jean Schlumberger, the first named designer at Tiffany, was commissioned early in his career by Elsa Schiaparelli to make jewel-like buttons for her clothes in 1937. 'Not one looked like what a button was supposed to look like', she said on seeing the chessmen, miniature mirrors, porcelain flowers and brightly coloured enamels for the first time. Schlumberger used his extraordinary vision to create collections of fanciful floral jewels, suspending chunks of finely cut semi-precious sapphires under delicate diamond florets, and sparking a floral trend among New York's most stylish women. The elegant American Babe Paley bought a necklace with golden bell-shaped tulips whose stems were lightly tied in a bow to elegant diamond leaves. Jacqueline Kennedy was given a Schlumberger ruby and diamond 'berry' brooch by her husband for her first Christmas in the White House, and Mrs Nathaniel Hill, the Campbell's soup heiress, commissioned a multi-layered extravaganza of diamond buds and flowers on a garland of platinum leaves.

Floral Jewels

Nature has been an endless source of inspiration in jewellery design throughout the last century. During the Belle Époque both Chaumet and Boucheron created realistic, white diamond-set flowers mounted on spring-set diamond stems *en tremblant*, lending them a gentle swaying movement. The 1940s' styles were more colourful: golden rondelles alternated with rubies and bristling brilliant-cut diamonds bursting out of the top of a Cartier thistle, or a gold polished anemone flower head with petals curled back to reveal a ruby cabochon. Fashion houses have always cross-pollinated their floral motifs. Coco Chanel loved the camellia (the first flower given to her by her English love, 'Boy' Capel), sprinkling it over dresses, accessories and jewels. Each season the flower appears afresh in fabric, velvet and leather as well as rare electric blue Paraiba tourmaline brooches and black-and-white diamond rings. In 1954 Christian Dior crated a whole collection devoted to the lily-of-the-valley, inspired by his childhood garden in Normandy. Today this has been re-interpreted by jewellery designer Victoire de Castellane into a delicate diamond and emerald spray that wraps around the neck. Van Cleef & Arpels express the essence of different gardens in their floral jewels. The streams and lawns of a romantic English garden, for example, are evident in the emerald drop *Revele* ear clips with diamond foliage against green buds of plants glistening in the dawn dew. The supple collar of the *Versailles* necklace has undulating curves of pink and yellow diamonds like the flowerbeds by the grand flowing fountains at the chateau itself; while an Italian Renaissance garden is represented by the 45-carat peridot *Castello* ring surrounded by cabochon fruit rubies and diamond-set leaves.

Above: Black diamond 'Camélia' brooch by Chanel Fine Jewellery.
Below left: Diorissimo necklace by Christian Dior.
Centre top: Belladonna brooch by Christian Dior.
Centre bottom: Floral brooch by Van Cleef & Arpels.
Below right: Jardin des Hespérides necklace by Van Cleef & Arpels.

Above: Gold, emerald and ruby flower brooch, Trabert & Hoeffer, Mauboussin, Reflection, c. 1945.
Top left: Brooch by Chopard.
Top right: Boboli bracelet by H. Stern.
Centre: Lys bracelet by Lorenz Bäumer. Sapphires, chalcedony, amethyst, iolite, silvolite, 18ct white gold.

Just as the florals on fashionable fabrics change over time so too the heritage-style blooms of bejewelled Belle Époque roses and peonies have been swept away in favour of more modern, exotic blooms. Asprey creates pink sapphire-studded calla lilies, and in the voluptuous-looking orchids at Cartier diamond petals are peppered with dustings of yellow sapphire pollen on graduating green garnet stems with red rubellites spilling out of the orchid's central trumpet. Shaun Leane also creates orchids with an edge. Not wanting to focus on 'the girly association with the flower shape', he replaces the central stamen of the bloom with a tusk. H. Stern may have used the ancient Boboli Gardens at the Pitti Palace as inspiration for their *Boboli* collection, but for a modern audience the style is less botanically accurate, using exuberant slivers of gold cut and crushed into organic floral shapes. 'It's old-fashioned to mimic nature too closely', says Jeremy Morris at David Morris, of his exuberant sapphire and diamond-leaf brooches. 'Instead, I take a likeness. An idea of a flower.'

1   Titanium, spinel and diamond brooch, Adler.
2   White diamond 'Camélia' brooch, Chanel Fine Jewellery.
3   Diamond and ruby earrings, Cartier.
4   Lucite and crystal brooch, Alexis Bittar at Liberty.
5   Antique Gold, enamel, saphire and turquoise brooch, Van Cleef & Arpels.
6   Amethyst, sapphire and tsavorite brooch, Asprey.
7   Gold, tsavorite and diamond brooch, Calleija.
8   Diamond and conch-pearl brooch, Moussaieff.
9   Tsavorite and diamond earrings, Glenn Spiro.
10 Diamond and pearl brooch, Tiffany.
11 Tsavorite, sapphire, diamond and pearl brooch, David Morris.
12 Diamond and ruby brooch, Cartier.
13 Antique diamond and ruby brooch, Van Cleef and Arpels.
14 Titanium and diamond brooch, Chopard.
15 Sapphire, ruby and diamond brooch, Adler.
16 Diamond ring, Leviev.
17 Titanium and diamond brooch, Moussaieff.
18 Gold, turquoise and tourmaline ring, Dior Joaillerie.

> *'The clothes that I prefer are those I invent for a life that doesn't exist yet, the world of tomorrow.'*
> Pierre Cardin

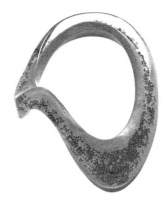

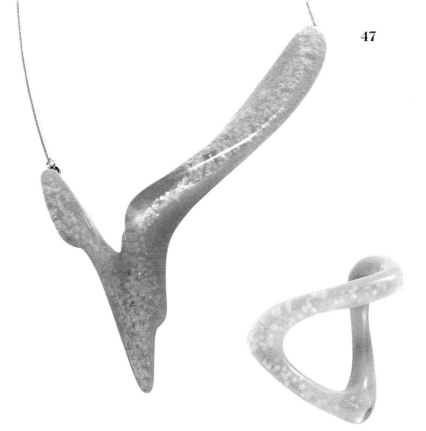

Fantasy Futures

Futuristic style uses high-tech fabrics such as rubber, metal and white vinyl to create designs with a dash of science-fiction fantasy. In the 1960s, when the world was intrigued by space travel and the Soviets and Americans raced to be first on the moon, André Courrèges was the first designer known for his futuristic look — all-white trapeze shapes, PVC mini-skirts and space helmets. He used vinyl and silver fabrics and moulded plastic visors onto astronaut-style hats. During the 1980s Thierry Mugler innovated a futuristic-meets-Hollywood trend of rounded hips, sharply accented shoulders with an intergalactic warrior chic drawn from movies such as *Mad Max* or *The Terminator*.

In tune with today's uncertainty about the future of the environment Alexander McQueen created a post-apocalyptic collection of reptile-patterned printed dresses shown on alien-like models teetering in 12-inch platforms shaped like scaly armadillo heads. Futuristic in execution as well as appearance, the prints were the work of computer-generated art, forecasting a watery amphibian future for humans beings after the ice-caps have melted. Gareth Pugh has created his own retro-futuristic style using new century fabrics such as Perspex patchwork, metal mesh shifts, rubber body stockings and masks in designs which reference the past. He mixes Elizabethan high-necked concertina ruffles, with his trademark science-fiction-style shoulders and articulated limbs, which swoop in arcs from neck to knee and in a giant 'V' rising from the waist to obscure the face. Oversized avant-garde perspex, plastic, acrylic and resin jewellery, like shiny spaceship cuffs and rings, fits with the futuristic style alongside silver medieval-style breastplates for the warrior look. Shaun Leane creates silver body pieces like large metal cages that seem to float in mid-air around the body. Bagdad-born architect Zaha Hadid designs swooping cuffs, rings and necklaces in sinuous modern forms with colourful crystals suspended in clear resin to make a futuristic statement.

Top: Glace bangles and Celeste necklace by Zaha Hadid for Atelier Swarovski.
Centre: 18ct rose gold ring with platinum, conch pearl and diamonds by Atelier Zobel.
Above: Shaun Leane for Alexander McQueen, spring/summer 2008.

Above: Acrylic brooch
by Adam Paxon.
Below left: Hinged loop neckpiece
by David Watkins, 1974. Dyed acrylic
and silver.
Below centre: Pendant necklace
by David Watkins, 1974. Dyed acrylic
and gold.
Below right: A Paco Rabanne
dress made up of linked plastic
squares, 1967.

Paco Rabanne (1934–)

Space age was the word used to describe the influential and eccentric clothes designed by Paco Rabanne in the 1960s when he set the world of fashion alight experimenting with seamless dresses made by spraying vinyl chloride into moulds. Unlike the traditional couturier's sewing equipment Rabanne used industrial implements such as pliers and a blowtorch to fashion his simple shift mini-dresses in triangles of aluminium and pieces of scrap metal. He used matte silver leather for capes and created the first disposable dress in paper and nylon thread which resembled a Sputnik prototype for a moon landing. He showed his clothes with bib necklaces which he made in primary-coloured plastic discs strung together with fine wire.

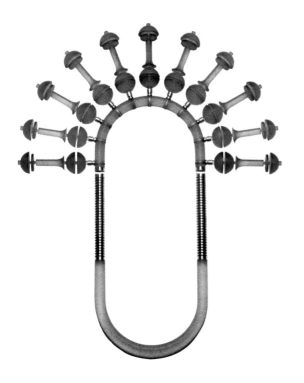

Lady Gaga (1986–)

Like Paco Rabanne American singer Lady Gaga favours high-tech materials such as shiny black PVC catsuits, latex leggings, mirrored mini-dresses and thick plastic worn with vinyl lace-up white boots for her eccentric outfits. Fractured disco balls appear as garments with gimp masks or intergalactic sculptured silver hats with white diamante mini-dresses, or gold and sequin Granny pants worn as lingerie-style outer wear. In her *Bad Romance* video Lady Gaga wears Alexander McQueen's futuristic armadillo-style extreme platforms, and attaches several large metal hoops which appear to rotate around her silver lurex body like shiny satellites. A celestial-style lilac-coloured Armani Privé gown with Swarovski crystals glitters around her like a swirling solar system which she wears with bejewelled platforms and carries a sputnik-like stick like a jewelled wand. One of Lady Gaga's inspirations is rock star David Bowie, as his 1970s' alter ego Ziggy Stardust. 'It was a cross between Nijinsky and Woolworths', Bowie said about his brightly coloured one-piece jumpsuits worn with glitter and thunderbolt make-up.

Top left: Lady Gaga, 2010.
Top right: Pastille and Astrale rings by Lorenz Bäumer.
Above: David Bowie, c. 1970.

Bejewelled Fashion

'A ball dress might be entirely covered with millions of paillettes, or pearls, each one of which has to be put on separately.'

Christian Dior

When used as part of clothing jewellery originally had the practical function of fastening the garment as well as being a form of embellishment. During the Renaissance high collars and mufflers were encrusted with gemstones and Tudor England was awash with vast quantities of pearls which took seamstresses days to sew onto elaborately embroidered bodices and trains. During the 1950s fine silk organza evening gowns might be decorated with semi-precious stones, silver sequins, metallic thread, beads, ostrich feathers and crystals, in an embroidering process that could take up to a month.

In 2002 to showcase the decorative art of the ateliers in Paris who add the glitz and glitter to clothes with beading, embroidery and jewelled handwork Karl Lagerfeld founded the Chanel Métiers d'Art collection. Today Lagerfeld's Chanel Couture shows can almost match the Tudor court in the pomp and display of jewelled clothes. One gothic-style tunic top was a mass of jewelled crosses and crystal medallions linked together like a modern chain-mail vest. It has been estimated that a massive 450,000 sequins and pearls, in a myriad of different beading techniques, shine on the exquisitely flounced tulle extravaganzas of a Chanel collection.

At Gucci creative director Frida Giannini, an accessories expert, designed embroidered evening wear in a palette of jewel hues with large brooches sewn into the fabric made from amethysts, agate and crystal to hold the gowns together. Her iconic Little Black Dresses in crepe de chine are given a touch of rock-and-roll with metal and crystal embroidery and jewel-like harnesses in silver and crystal with black metal beading.

Top left: Choker by Dior.
Top right: Necklace by Louis Vuitton.
Above: Gucci, spring/summer 2010.
Opposite: Chanel haute couture, spring/summer 2010.

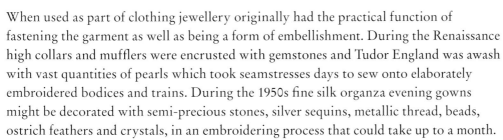

Alber Elbaz (1961–)

The oldest couture house in Paris, the House of Lanvin, created by Jeanne Lanvin in 1889, is known for ornamental embellishment such as beading, appliqué and embroidery. A typical 1930s-style Lanvin chiffon and tulle evening gown would be stitched with black beaded bands in graduated scallops from bodice to hem. The current creative designer Alber Elbaz has taken this style of unabashed femininity a stage further combining fabrics with jewels into one glittering concoction. 'I introduced fabric to jewellery, wrapping pearls in tulle', he says, 'and fastening necklaces with grosgrain ribbon'. Jeanne Lanvin was never without her pearls and Elbaz whips up *faux* pearls into wispy modern fantasies with feathers and enamel beads on chains or wraps them seductively in black netting. Triple gold ring necklaces are tied with pretty silk ribbons, trench coats trimmed with diamante-studded ribbon and dark crystal necklace bibs become part of a silk tulle bodice on a Little Black Dress.

Above: Lanvin, winter 2010.
Below left: Royal blue, shocking orange or green pearls and silk strands by Lanvin.
Below right: Bird and strawberry Acapulco necklace by Lanvin.
Bottom left: Black, orange, red Fraise choker and red Fraise earrings by Lanvin.

Daniel Swarovski (1852–1956)

Over a hundred years ago Daniel Swarovski moved to a village in Austria with his newly invented machine for cutting and polishing crystal cut stones. In 1895 couturier Charles Worth, royal dressmaker to Empress Eugénie of France, used these Tyrolean cut stones for decorative effects on evening dresses. Swarovski has an impressive heritage of working with couturiers. Coco Chanel and Elsa Schiaparelli both used Swarovski crystal beads for trimmings, and for Christian Dior's costume jewels they created the Aurora Borealis stone shot through with glinting rainbow colours similar to an opal. Since 2004 the Atelier Swarovski has begun supporting a new generation of young designers who fuse fashion and jewellery, sculpting crystal into garments, embroidery and jewellery. In the hands of Giles Deacon crystals become a puff of tulle on a prom-style skirt, a bondage-style metallic corset or appliquéd onto soft grey felt neckpieces. Matthew Williamson's passion for prints and animated geometric designs are evident in the aesthetic of his oversized graphic cuffs and breastplate necklaces which use hexagonal and triangular-shaped crystal in a vibrant palette of orange, pink, green and blue. For Viktor & Rolf the Atelier created a method of laser striping crystals for a jewellery collection that coordinates with their densely bejewelled mini-dresses in red, black and pink rows of beads with pleats and whirling rosettes at the shoulder.

Top left: Necklace by Giles Deacon for Atelier Swarovski.
Top right: Cuffs by Matthew Williamson for Atelier Swarovski.
Centre: Earrings by Viktor & Rolf for Atelier Swarovski.

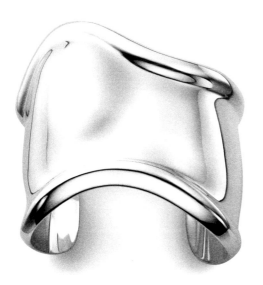

'Simplicity is the ultimate sophistication.'

Leonardo da Vinci

Back to Basics

Minimalism strips a garment down to its fundamental features to create simple, strong-shaped dresses with superbly executed, clean-cut lines in a neutral or quiet palette. Considered 'anti-fashion' the minimalist look can be so pared down and unadorned that it appears austere. But its strength lies in its simplicity. Practitioners of the art, such as Jil Sander, Donna Karan and Helmut Lang, keep the style unfussy and sculptural, cutting out any unnecessary seams, details, flounces or frills. Arguably the king of understatement is Calvin Klein, who began designing in 1968. He was inspired to design clean-lined dresses by the style of young New Yorkers. 'It's a philosophy', he said, 'that involves an overall sense of balance, knowing when to take away, subtract'. He also practised restraint on the catwalk, choosing similar-looking models wearing minimal make-up with either scraped-back chignons or long straight Ivy-League-style tresses. The basic shape of a kimono in traditional Japanese design has also been a source of inspiration for less-is-more advocates such as Jean Muir, who added pin-tucking and drapery to strong, clean shapes, echoing the lines of kimonos. It is a dedicated and disciplined design which eschews any decorative effects. What constitutes clutter to a true minimalist such as lace, fringing and jewels is considered embellishment by any other.

   For purists during the 1990s even a tiny diamond ear stud was considered *de trop*. The emphasis on restrained luxury over obvious ostentation led to a fashion for small stones discreetly threaded onto invisible wire like brilliant floating diamond dots. The subtle minimalist design of Elsa Peretti's bone-shaped cuff for Tiffany suited the uncluttered look, as its sleek contours followed a woman's wrist perfectly, becoming part of her body rather than a glamorous accessory which might detract from stylistic purity.

Top left: Bone cuff in sterling silver by Elsa Peretti for Tiffany & Co.
Top centre: Ring by Belmacz.
Top right: Cuff by Alexandra Jefford.
Above: Jil Sander, autumn/winter 2007.

Carolyn Bessette Kennedy (1966–99)

The photograph of Carolyn Bessette Kennedy wearing a silk pearl-coloured crepe wedding gown, designed by her friend Narciso Rodriguez, on her marriage to John Kennedy Jr. in 1996, defined her public persona as an icon of minimalist style. In a silky sheath with her hair loosely tied in a chignon and no other adornment Carolyn had honed her restrained look while working as a public relations executive for Calvin Klein in New York. Her black urban-chic wardrobe favoured slightly sculpted Yohji Yamamoto jackets and stark white shirts with pointed collars. It became the fashion to be imitated just as the pill-box hats and Empire-line shifts of Jacqueline Kennedy had been thirty years earlier. Even for a black-tie evening gala event Carolyn would eschew any glitz or glitter, preferring a sophisticated white wool dress with sleeves down to her wrists by Versace, a slash of red lipstick as her only colour accent.

Top left: Carolyn Bessette Kennedy and John Kennedy Jr., on their wedding day.
Top right: Cuffs by Alexandra Jefford.
Above: Party pavé ring by Jacqueline Rabun.

Vivianna Torun Bülow-Hübe (1927–2004)

Vivianna Torun Bülow-Hübe was a Swedish silversmith who designed at Georg Jensen from the mid-1950s. Her fluid asymmetric forms in silver had a unique sculpted simplicity and were created with a minimalist design directive. Early clients Brigitte Bardot and Ingrid Bergman were drawn to her shiny silver torques hung with polished pebbles in moonstone, rock crystal and quartz as well as her radical theories on jewellery: 'Diamonds have a killing effect on woman's beauty', she said. While living on the French Riviera and wandering along the shore collecting pebbles for her jewels Torun Bülow-Hübe first met Pablo Picasso, who wore her beach-pebble cuff links. She fashioned large collars dripping with lead crystal pendants: 'It's a style of ornamentation we know in Scandinavia from the Viking neckbands and it's part of our heritage', she said. She encapsulated life and movement in her twirling *Whirl* earrings and sensual, organic-shaped *Möbius* brooches, designed to fit the contours of a woman's body perfectly. She created the first watch from Georg Jensen using a minimalist aesthetic, fashioning an open-sided bangle with a simple mirror-like watch face, and stripping the design of all but the bare essentials — including any numbers on the dial.

Top: Stainless steel wristwatch, 1966 by Bülow-Hübe.
Above: Möbius brooch in sterling silver by Bülow-Hübe.
Below left: Silver necklace by Bülow-Hübe.
Below right: Bülow-Hübe with Picasso in Antibes.

*'Nothing gives
the luxury of pearls.'*

Diana Vreeland

Power Pearls

Monarchs and potentates have always made pearls a symbol of their status and prestige. Queen Elizabeth I, who wore seven or more ropes of pearls together, some extending as low as her knees, used the power pearl look to define her regal status. The finest giant pear-shaped pearl in the world, La Peregrina, found by a slave diving off the coat of Panama in 1560, has been the prized possession of a string of monarchs from Philip II of Spain to Mary, Queen of Scots. It currently nestles in the décolletage of movie queen Elizabeth Taylor. Power pearls are a safe political choice because they project an image of success and classy refinement, rather than sex appeal, making them the perfect adornment for residents of the White House. Successive US First Ladies such as Jacqueline Kennedy, Barbara Bush and Hillary Clinton have used pearls to accessorise their Oscar de La Renta suits and Cassini shift dresses for a working-chic look. Michelle Obama is making globular pearls her signature style, mixing them with a sleeveless purple crepe sheath dresses by Maria Pinto as easily as a Jason Wu teal skirt and Junya Watanabe cardigan. Not only do pearls enhance the authoritative air of the working woman but it has been scientifically proven that they capture light, illuminating the face *d'un certain âge* with a flattering sheen.

Top left: Pearl necklace by Coleman and Douglas.
Top right: Perle et noeud ring by Chanel Fine Jewellery.
Above: US First Lady Michelle Obama, 2009.

The Queen Mother (1900–2002)

After the luxurious diamond-clustered reign of her mother-in-law, Queen Mary, pearls enabled the young Elizabeth to create her own, simpler style. During the Queen Mother's youth she wore flapper-length double pearl chains with 1920s' diamond bandeaux or diamond-fringed tiaras. During the war, with the royal jewels wrapped in newspaper and stored in a vault at Windsor Castle, Queen Elizabeth wore shorter strands of pearls which she considered less showy and a more appropriate jewel to wear. On holidays in Scotland she wore a rope of pearls as comfortably with a kilt designed by Norman Hartnell as at an evening reception with a green chartreuse-coloured dress with net sleeves and elaborate silver embroidery. In later life she wore a series of brightly coloured coats with matching dresses, so the public could see her from a distance, pinned with her favourite Jubilee brooch, a pearl-and-diamond floral brooch with a pearl centre and drop, which had been presented to Queen Victoria by her household in 1837. As *Vogue* wrote in 1969: 'Think of how pearls glow in praise of skin… long ropes of pearls, round or baroque, creamy white, pale pink or silver, cool and luminous as moonlight', a description which sums up the fashion style of a veritable 'Pearly Queen'.

Top left: Pearl necklace by Bulgari.
Top centre: Pearl sash clip by Mikimoto, reissued in 1934.
Top right: South Sea pearl necklace by Autore.
Above: Hand-coloured portrait of Queen Elizabeth, 1937.

South Sea Pearls

The South Sea pearls found in the warm clear waters around Australia, Tahiti and the other islands in French Polynesia (home of the *Pinctada maxima* mollusc) make the ultimate power pearls because of their size. At least ten millimetres in diameter with a flawless lustre and perfect white hue, their gentle roundness and perfect form convey softness as well as strength. Coco Chanel was passionate about pearls, mixing them with all textures of fabric from tweed to fluid silks and even sportswear. In 1924 she sanctioned the use of *faux* pearls to achieve the over-sized South Sea look for a fraction of the price. The models at Chanel shows still flaunt ropes of shiny white fakes, in dramatic sizes, slung and knotted around their waists, wrists and necks in graduating lengths. Their fine pearl sautoirs have frosted droplets delicately suspended from diamond stems of camellias or pearls set into spiralling swirls of diamonds. Autore, the world's largest South Sea pearl company, creates fashion extravaganzas, setting pearls like marine treasures in underwater scenes of diamonds, sapphire, tsavorites, aquamarines and blue Paraiba tourmalines, tangled together like seaweed.

Above: US First Lady Jackie Kennedy, 1962.
Below far left: Pearl ring by Chopard.
Below centre: Necklace by Autore.
Bottom left: Earrings by Autore.
Bottom right: Multicoloured pearls, sapphires and diamonds 'Swing' brooch by Chanel Fine Jewellery.

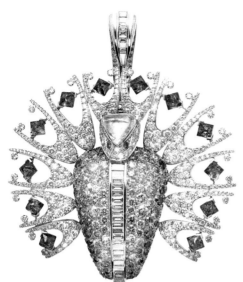

'21st-century chic modern style warriors.'

Julia Muggenburg

Tribal Glamour

North-African-born Yves Saint Laurent was the first designer to adapt styles from tribal cultures for haute couture. In the 1960s he created slinky brown African-print dresses, turbans and tunics made from latticed wooden beads, raffia dresses and conical-shaped bras made out of shells. It has inspired other designers too: the silk mini-dresses by Alber Elbaz for Lanvin, for example, were held around the neck by rows of pleated metallic fabric inspired by traditional Masai outfits. Designers now use luxurious accessories to lend tribal references to collections such as the colourful wrist bangles at Diane von Furstenberg made by local artisans in South Africa from recycled telephone wire. The warm-coloured draped jersey dresses by Amanda Wakeley were weighed down with large serpentine ringed chokers by Maria Francesco Pepe, lying like coiled snakes wrapped around the models' necks. Satin turbans worn with heavy suede pieces embroidered with African tribal art by Miuccia Prada created an *Out of Africa* look mixed with a frisson of 1940s' glamorous gowns in jewel-like colours. The touches of African razzle-dazzle at Louis Vuitton have been added by huge hooped earrings, beaded necklaces, shoes with feathered and tasselled ankle straps, gold metallic clutch bags tied with a rope hung with resin and metal pompoms. Dutch-born Bibi van der Velden makes modern sculptured rings out of 40,000-year-old mammoth bone found in the Siberian permafrost which she carves into animal-head rings studded with semi-precious stones and pearls. Bulgari have created strands of turquoise, amethyst and emeralds with white gold rondelles specifically to accessorise the African tribal look; and Shaun Leane makes tribal-meets-Deco-style onyx beads in long lariats hung from diamond and green tsavorite tusks with tassels.

Above left: King Cobra pendant by De Beers.
Above right: Necklace by Shaun Leane.

Above: Bangles by Catherine Noll.
Below left: Peridot and pockwood
necklace by Hemmerle.
Below right: Tourmaline, pockwood
and white gold bangle by Hemmerle.
Centre right: Bangle in carbon set
with diamonds by Adler.
Bottom: Bangle tower by Belmacz.

Wood

Wood jewellery makes its wearers feel connected to the earth and nature. Designer Julia Muggenburg makes cult wooden cuffs, like status-confirming tribal trophies. Using woods from around the world such as mopani from South Africa, Brazilian tabebuia, wenge from Congo, Scottish burr elm and English holly she creates bangles in a variety of shapes with gold detailing. Catherine Noll inherited a workshop full of ivory and rare woods from her grandfather, Parisian furniture maker Alexandre Noll, where she made sculptural pieces in the 1970s. Ebony and ivory bangles, mother-of-pearl and rosewood breastplates were mixed with clear acrylic to give a graphic, African look. Wood in the hands of fourth-generation German jewellers Hemmerle becomes a piece of haute joaillerie. With sophisticated understatement they polish rare amaranth into a bangle, set in the centre with a brilliant blue amethyst or lime-green garnet, or use a rare, vivid orange melo pearl with tagua nut like a precious acorn.

African Masks

As the French Empire expanded into Africa before World War I tribal artefacts were bought back to Paris and came to influence the Cubist movement, most famously in Picasso's 1907 painting *Les Demoiselles d'Avignon* where the women's facial features are visibly disintegrating into primitive masks. Picasso approached jewellery design as a work of art to be displayed as well as worn and his gold-worked designs of eyes or faces are abstract forms of modern masks. Louis Vuitton has used plastic collages of abstract African faces on shoes as tribal references. Diamond jewellers De Beers looked back to their century-long African association to create the *Amulet* collection, weaving African folklore stories of spirits into rings and pendants encrusted with diamonds and talismanic properties of good luck redolent of ancient tribal masks.

Top left and right: Pendants by De Beers.
Centre and above: Masks by Butler & Wilson.

Post-War Classics

*'The damson jam of the velvet, bordered with
the clotted cream of ermine and sprinkled with
the sugar of diamonds.'*

Norman Hartnell on the peeresses at the 1953 coronation

Classic style in the 1950s was a celebration of elegance and femininity that had been lost during the war years. Parisian haute couture dominated fashion: Cristóbal Balenciaga broadened women's shoulders, removed their waists, and created the tunic dress which progressed into Empire-line high-waisted dresses and coats cut like a Japanese kimono. Women looking for luxury after the hardships of rationing found that diamonds were available again in abundance. Although one of the most iconic images of the time was Marilyn Monroe, singing 'Diamonds are a Girl's Best Friend' in the film *Gentlemen Prefer Blondes*, the greatest influence on diamond fashions came from Queen Elizabeth II. The scale and opulence of the diamond regalia worn by the Queen and her courtiers at the coronation in 1953 were so impressive that fine jewellers around the world set out to emulate the impact of a royal diamond. The regal diamonds were worn in matching suites to maximise impact: huge pear- and marquise-cut diamonds with comparable bracelets and rings, and diamond drops shimmering from earlobes with historic diadems dazzling on top of aristocratic heads.

Following this trend Jacqueline Kennedy wore an Empire-line Givenchy silk evening gown with circular Van Cleef & Arpels diamond *Flammes* brooches, and diamond ear-clips with a wheatsheaf clip across the top of her hair like a whiff of a royal tiara. The modern classicism of Dolce & Gabbana, focussing on the 1950s-style heritage-chic of kilts, tweed, Hermès scarves and painted organza fantasy ball gowns has been inspired by the Queen as a contemporary fashion icon. Van Cleef & Arpels also drew on post-war classics in the creation of their diamond and platinum *744 Fifth* collection for 21ˢᵗ-century women looking for supple swirls of marquise-cut diamonds and cascades of diamonds hung with luminous pearl-shaped drops similar to necklaces that would have been worn in the 1950s by diamond patrons such as Doris Duke and Paulette Goddard.

Top: White and pink tiara by Graff.
Above: Dolce & Gabbana, autumn/winter 2008/09.

Laurence Graff (1938–)

Laurence Graff, known worldwide as the King of Diamonds, began making jewellery as a 15-year-old apprentice in London's Hatton Garden. Born with the 1950s' sensibility for maximising the impact of a diamond, Graff was an early advocate of 'bling', setting one of the first rings he made with 33 very small diamonds to create the biggest flash possible. His pieces are deceptively simple in design terms, with nothing to detract attention from the beauty of the stones. Good-sized fancy-cut diamonds, egg-sized canary yellow diamonds or magnificent 'D'-coloured flawless stones are 'knitted' into discreet wire mountings. The sensuality and fluidity of 1950s' fashion is mirrored in Graff's jewels. 'When a woman moves', says Laurence Graff, 'you can see the stones shimmer and move too'. White-tie formal 1950s-style dressing lives on at Graff, who creates modern tiaras for royal Middle Eastern weddings and grand balls, including a pink diamond piece for the Queen of Brunei.

Andrew Grima (1921–2007)

While the Queen wore her historic tiaras and formal diamonds her sister, Princess Margaret, embraced new design and avant-garde jewellery. She was an early patron of Andrew Grima, the leader of the post-war English modernist jewellery movement, who revolutionised fine jewellery. He moved away from the forms and materials of classic jewels to experiment with organic shapes, *objets trouvés*, textured wire and exotic rough-cut semi-precious stones and crystals. 'A 50-carat topaz can become art', he said, 'it's not about the monetary value. A 50-carat diamond should be in a bank vault'. Moving the emphasis away from precious stones, Grima could create a piece of wearable sculpture from a pile of twigs and leaves. Princess Margaret sent him a piece of lichen, picked up on a walk in Scotland, which he cast in gold as a brooch and pair of earrings. He set large grey South Sea pearls into gold, textured to resemble tree bark, or randomly dotted emeralds and sapphires cut like tiny geometric ice cubes around a large Australian black opal. This modernist jewellery chimed with the new mood in fashion as the century hurtled towards the Swinging Sixties.

Top: Necklace and brooches by Grima.
Above: *Princess Margaret wearing a Grima brooch, 2005.*

Disco Queens

'*Decarnin certainly proved he's the leader of the disco fever he has single-handedly triggered this season. He has the shortest, tightest body dresses witnessed anywhere; smothered in Swarovski crystals, flouncing up at the shoulder, tightly bound in satin drape or quilted, chain-wrapped black leather.*'

Sarah Mower

The lush, electric sound of 1970s' New York nightclubs, with their trippy lighting and new free-form dances such as *The Hustle*, created distinct new fashions for both men and women. The film *Saturday Night Fever*, starring John Travolta, began a trend for light-coloured suits over shiny shirts with pointy collars open at the neck to reveal golden medallion chains. For women it triggered a dancewear-inspired look, as disco fashion was primarily created to look good on the dance floor. Clothes were adapted from modern professional dance-wear used in the dance studios that had sprung up in the city. Leotards worn with wraparound rayon or jersey skirts became an important fashion accessory for women dancing on high platform heels under strobe lights. Swirling, patterned fabrics in newly invented psychedelic-coloured polyester were inspired by glam-rock performers such as Marc Bolan of T. Rex. Sonny-and-Cher-style jumpsuits matched faces sparkling with glitter, false eyelashes fluttering above layers of blue eye shadow and glamorous diamanté hoops with long loose gold chains to define the disco look. Fabrics such as gold lamé, satin and velvet jackets, shiny Lycra and stretch sequin were worn to reflect the light bouncing off mirrored disco balls and ultra-violet lighting.

Nostalgia for nightclub fashion is evident in the glossy jackets, super-glam crystal-studded minis and sexy party dresses of contemporary collections by Marc Jacobs, Antonio Beradi and Donatella Versace. New York jeweller Ivanka Trump shines in metallic fabrics and disco balls, while Fawaz Gruosi's disco-ball necklaces and earrings rotate with dazzling diamonds.

Top left and right: Earrings and necklace by De Grisogono. **Above:** Gucci, autumn/winter 2006.

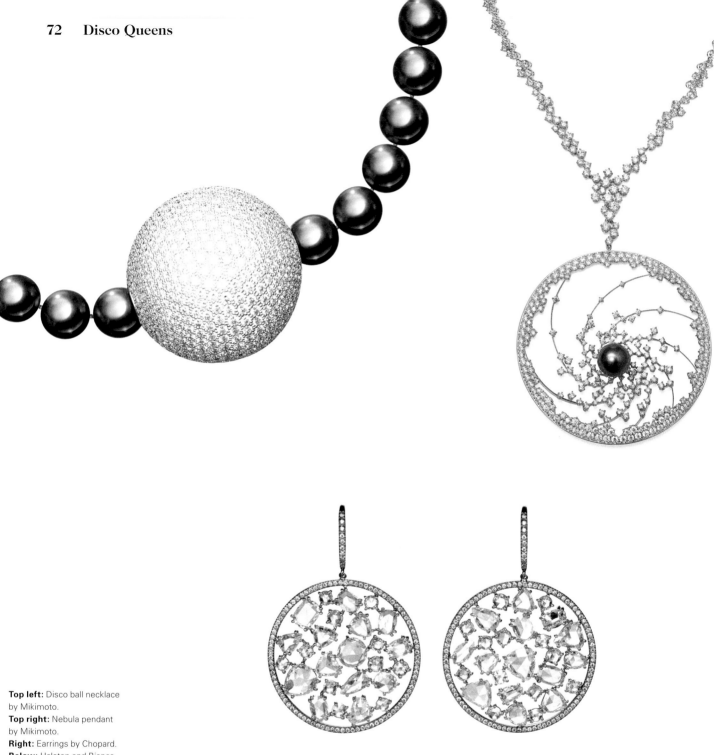

Top left: Disco ball necklace by Mikimoto.
Top right: Nebula pendant by Mikimoto.
Right: Earrings by Chopard.
Below: Halston and Bianca Jagger, 1980.

Halston (1932–90)

Fashion designer Halston lived the celebrity lifestyle alongside the 1970s' icons he dressed such as Bianca Jagger and Liza Minnelli. His trademark technique was to create evening clothes with the concept of comfort and relaxation, and his signature slinky halter-neck styles and draped jersey dresses, inspired by classical Roman and Greek dress, became the new party wear. His kaftans, dusty coloured djellabas, ultra-suede shirt-dresses and wide-legged pants made the perfect leisure wear for the 1970s. In spite of the simplicity of his design Halston was associated with the decadence and hedonistic glamour of Manhattan's infamous Studio 54 nightclub. The Halston name has today been given a modern makeover under creative director Marios Schwab and is incarnated by Sarah Jessica Parker, Carrie Bradshaw in the TV series *Sex and the City*.

Elsa Peretti (1940–)

Joining Tiffany as a named designer in 1974 Elsa Peretti swept away the concept of formal diamonds for special occasions and revolutionised the way women wore fine jewels. She wanted diamonds to be widely available to all women and so created a new casual look by sprinkling twelve small diamonds set into gold collets along a chain at uneven intervals. Her friend Halston immediately named it 'diamonds by the yard'. As *Newsweek* stated: 'What Peretti had was a whole new idea of what jewellery should be. No longer serious, real jewellery had become accessible and affordable for every secretary and shop girl'. With this diamond chain Peretti pioneered the contemporary concept of the all-day jewel. Unostentatious it created a glamorous sparkle for women to wear both to the office and then to the disco, without the fear of losing an important diamond. 'It was Studio 54', Peretti explained to *Mirabella* magazine, 'and you didn't want to lose anything'. Halston and Peretti shared the distinctive approach of creating simple comfortable shapes which they invested with a potent sensuality appealing to the sexually liberated woman of the 1970s. Halston made casual jersey dresses which clung to every curve of a woman's body, while Peretti's undulating, organic-shaped, bones, beans, snakes, teardrops and hearts in smooth, silver polished surfaces, Japanese lacquer, rock crystal or black jade wrapped seamlessly around her limbs and neck.

Above: Elsa Peretti.
Below left: Elsa Peretti® Diamonds By The Yard® for Tiffany & Co. Diamond necklace in 18ct gold.
Below right: Lacquer pendants by Elsa Peretti for Tiffany & Co.

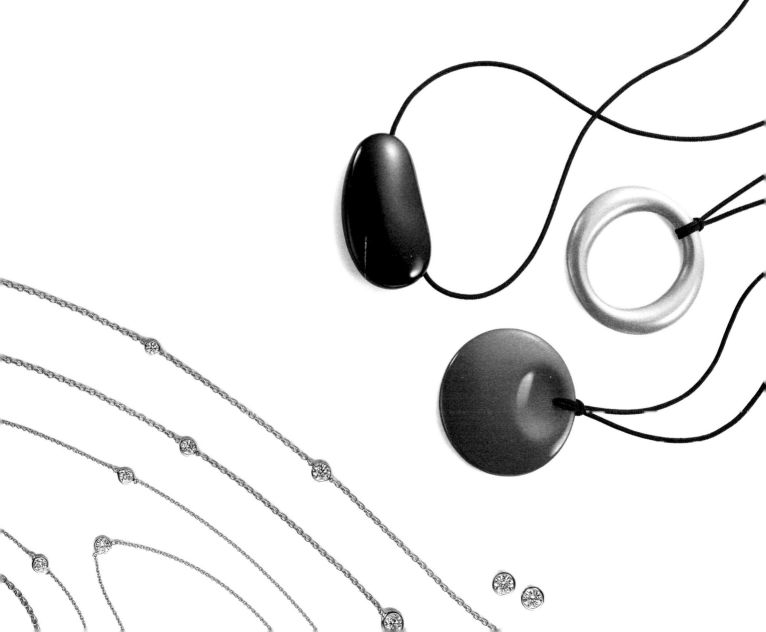

Artistic Jewels

'I've always liked painters. It seems to me that we are in the same trade and that they are my colleagues.'

Paul Poiret

Above: Frames by Cora Sheibani.
Below: Water Ring in 22ct gold and green enamel by Anish Kapoor.
Bottom: Dolce & Gabbana, spring/summer 2008.

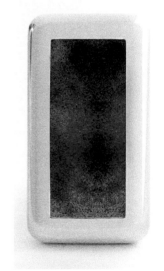

Art has influenced fashion and jewels since the powerful impact of the Surrealists on fashion during the 1930s. Elsa Schiaparelli worked with Salvador Dalí to create a skeleton dress, lamb-cutlet hat, veils embedded with crystal tears and an organdie lobster dress with parsley sprigs worn by the Duchess of Windsor prior to her marriage in 1937. Dalí's jewellery displayed the fetishism and fantasy of the Surrealist movement in his blood-red lip brooches, showing white pearl 'teeth', and starfish with articulated emerald, ruby and diamond arms which wrapped around hands like precious fingers. Today glimpses of Surrealism can be seen in the shows of Viktor & Rolf: their fantastical creations include models wearing cumbersome lighting structures, collars that appear to be attached to fluffy pillows and clothing presented upside-down.

The pioneers of modern art, Picasso, Max Ernst and Man Ray, all made jewellery. They downsized objects into wearable gold ornaments, reflecting their view that jewellery is a work of art to be displayed as well as worn. Renowned British jeweller, Wendy Ramshaw, was inspired by a Picasso pencil drawing of Françoise Gilot to create an oxidised silver-and-black acrylic neckpiece in 1988. Ramshaw said the shapes contained elements from the drawing, 'like a large rigid feather, another a black cloud suspended amongst zigzags and a spiral with a terminal…' In 1965 Yves Saint Laurent used the geometric works of Dutch abstract painter Piet Mondrian as inspiration for his iconic *Mondrian* shift dresses in red, white and blue blocks of colour; and the following year he launched a Pop art collection inspired by Andy Warhol and Roy Lichtenstein. More recently the white paint-splash effects on black sheer dresses used by Dolce & Gabbana and Michael Kors resemble the spontaneous 'drip' technique employed by Abstract Expressionist Jackson Pollock. 'I like to think that if Jackson Pollock were alive, and a fashion designer', says Kors, 'he would have come up with the black-and-white prints in the collection'. Of his lighter sea foam, pearl and lavender paint splashes he said: 'I love the Impressionist painters, and the colours and prints in this show reflect this'.

Above: The Trinity ring by Cartier.
Below: Jean Cocteau wearing his Trinity rings in 1951.
Below right: Design for Jean Cocteau's Academician sword, with its huge emerald given by Gabrielle Chanel, and sketch of the sword, Cartier Paris, 1955.

Jean Cocteau (1889–1963)

The French poet, novelist and film maker, Jean Cocteau, collaborated with both fashion and jewellery designers, admiring the direct approach such creativity afforded: 'Style', he said 'is a simple way of saying complicated things'. With Schiaparelli in 1937 he designed a jacket embroidered with a female figure: one hand caressed the waist of the wearer, while her long blonde hair cascaded down one sleeve. On another dress he had the profile of two faces embroidered and entwined to resemble a vase of flowers. During the 1920s he talked about creating the perfect jewel with his friend Louis Cartier and together they designed the cult *Trinity* ring of interlocking platinum with pink and yellow gold bands. Cocteau described Cartier as 'an artful magician, that masterfully balances slivers of moon on threads of sun'. Cocteau also worked with Boucheron, sketching an inventive golden scarf necklace bordered with rubies with a pearl and ruby 'knot' in the centre.

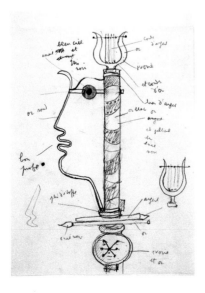

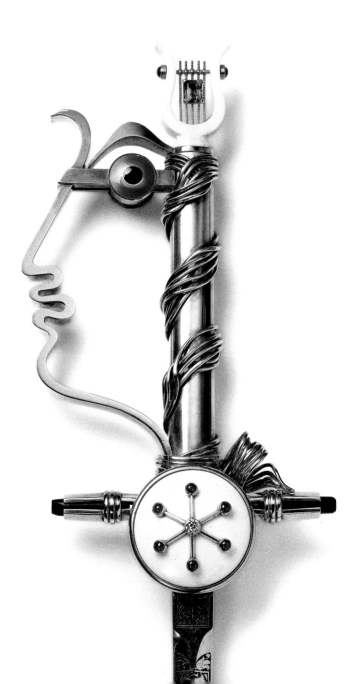

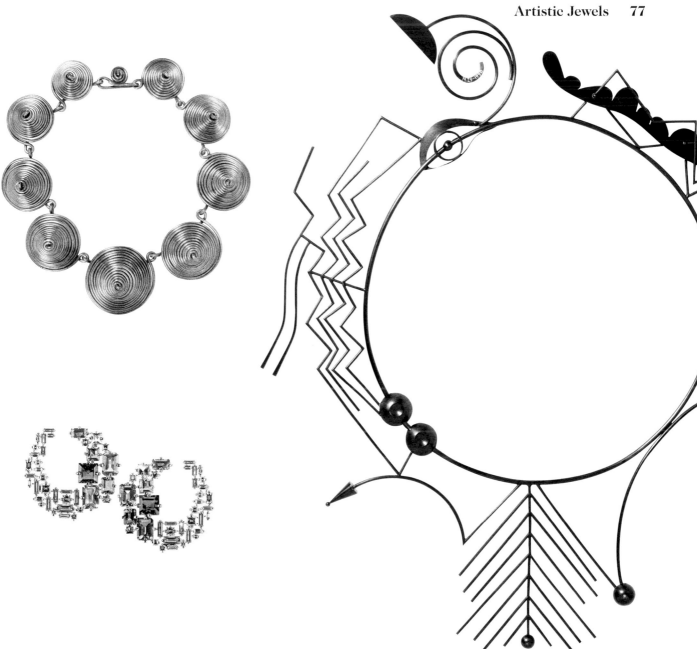

Jewelled Sculptures

It was a visit to Piet Mondrian's workshop in 1930, particularly a white wall covered in cardboard coloured rectangles, which inspired the artist Alexander Calder's turn to abstraction. His jewellery sculptures — floaty spheres, arcs and constellations suspended on wire — were named 'mobiles' by Marcel Duchamp and were soon worn by everyone in bohemian Paris at the time. The abstract forms of his jewellery, hand crafted by broadening and flattening steel, silver and brass wire, squiggled into leaves, circles and spirals, made them portable and wearable versions of his larger sculptures.

Turner Prize-winning artist Anish Kapoor creates *Slant* and *Water* jewels which resemble miniaturised versions of the work in his 2009 Royal Academy exhibition and play with similar concepts of coloured illusory voids and mirrored surfaces. The empty rectangular, oval and teardrop hollows have curvatures lined with coloured enamel or a mirror-like finish that is so smooth it is impossible to tell if it is an empty unfathomable space or a large coloured precious stone. *Unwearable Jewels* is how jeweller Solange Azagury-Partridge describes her first artistic exhibition in 2008 of opulent wall art. They echo her *Cosmic* rings, with mystic themes inlaid with hard and precious gemstones set on mink and framed in ebony.

Top left: Conical spirals of brass wire, joined together by brass loops by Alexander Calder.
Top right: Neckpiece for Picasso's Portrait of a Woman, 1988, by Wendy Ramshaw. Patinated silver and Colorcore.
Centre: Cubism earrings by Stefano Canturi.
Above: Eye plaque by Solange Azagury-Partridge.

Colour Blocking

*'We have splashed it with colour.
Forget your inhibitions and steep
your mind in it — for colour runs riot.'*

Harper's Bazaar, 1940

Colour blocking uses vivid mix-and-match blasts of colour to give a youthful energy to fashion and jewels. Elsa Schiaparelli, one of the earliest exponents, had a flair for unusual colour combinations, mixing turquoise linen with grape-purple piping, or a Little Black Dress colour blocked with a lime green coat or bright red stockings. During the 1960s Mod girls also colour blocked their legs — by this time they were wearing the all-in-one new style tights. The 1980s was a period of loud colour worn with confident broad shoulders and dynamic, big-styled hair. It was the perfect moment for Paloma Picasso, who burst into Tiffany in 1979, with her penchant for car-headlight-sized stones in assertive colours, set into large-scale jewellery which balanced 1980s' proportions. Dazzling kaleidoscopic sparks shone from her bright pink and green tourmalines, dazzling orange Mexican fire opals, or sky-blue aquamarines which had uniquely textured surfaces and set a trend for colour-blocked jewels. 'My nature pushes me into designing big pieces', she explained. Her diamond ribbon *Xs* necklace provided high-impact deep colour with its vibrant mix of tanzanites, tourmalines, peridots and aquamarines. Picasso used richly shaded rubellites so often they became known as 'Paloma's plums'.

In the 21st century colour blocking has been given a bold new dynamism by fashion designers who use acid greens, tangerines and neon yellows. Richard Nicoll showed pale grey trouser suits which looked as if they had been dipped in coral up to the lowest button of the blazer. His sleeveless tuxedo-style pink-and-coral blocked jackets open over pillar-box red and pink shift tops with electric pink silk trousers, giving the collection an 1980s-style power punch.

Top left: Bracelet by Bulgari.
Top centre: Multicoloured diamond bracelet by Graff.
Top right: Stoned necklace by Solange Azagury-Partridge.
Above: Paloma Picasso.
Below: Sugar Stack rings by Paloma Picasso for Tiffany & Co.

Theo Fennell (1951–)

Jewellery in 1970s Britain frequently clung onto heritage-style jewels. Fine jewellery was still following a 1950s-style formality using the limited colour palette of the Big Four gemstones; diamonds, sapphires, rubies and emeralds. Designer Theo Fennell bucked the trend by setting his flamboyant pieces in bold blocks of colour. 'Using just diamonds reduces your palette', said Fennell boldly. He introduced deep indigo-blue-shaded tanzanites and the electric aqua hue of the Paraiba tourmaline, which he described as 'the shade of a David Hockney swimming pool'. Fennell's store became a beacon of cutting-edge design fizzing with colour, as he created 'couture' pieces such as *Bombé* rings which flashed with florescent sapphires, gob-stopper sized minty green beryls and lozenge-shaped morganites.

Above: Theo Fennell.
Below left and right: 18ct yellow gold, peridot, citrine and pink tourmaline scattered cuff bangle and brooch by Theo Fennell.
Bottom: Bombé rings by Theo Fennell.

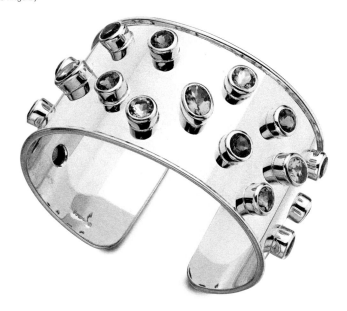

Coloured Diamonds

Monarchs have always had a penchant for a gulls-egg-sized coloured diamond. The dark blue 35.50-carat Wittelsbach diamond, for instance, was sold to Louis XIV of France then to Philip IV of Spain, bouncing down the ages from one royal owner to the next until it landed in the vaults of Laurence Graff. The Queen had the 24-carat Williamson pink diamond set by Cartier into a jonquil brooch with marquise-shaped diamond petals. Coloured diamonds arguably came into fashion at the end of the last century when a 0.95-carat red diamond was auctioned for one million dollars in New York. Realising how valuable coloured diamonds were, savvy jewellers began marketing brown diamonds (the colour most commonly found in diamonds and the earliest found in Roman rings) under the attractive names of 'cognac' and 'champagne', sparking a fashion for subtle, earthy shades. Large yellow, pink and blue diamonds remain exceptionally rare, so have become the jewellery accessory for movie stars wishing to set themselves apart. Nicole Kidman homogenised her look at the 2004 Academy Awards in green Chanel couture with 195 carats of green diamonds set into pink gold by Bulgari. To accept the Best Actress statuette at the 2001 Oscars Halle Berry wore shimmering blue with four million dollars worth of blue-and-white Harry Winston diamonds including a 30-carat blue diamond pendant.

Top left: Yellow diamond necklace by Graff.
Top centre: Orange diamond ring by De Beers.
Top right: Necklace of square emerald-cut light pink diamond, multicoloured diamonds, marquise-shaped pink diamonds, square-emerald, oval and marquise-shaped diamonds, pink diamonds by Leviev.
Above: The 5.11ct trilliant-cut Moussaieff Red Diamond. The Wittelsbach diamond at Graff.

Bohemian Rhapsodies

'The gypsy look … flourished amongst the young attending pop festivals: calico, big leather belts, beads, shawls, handkerchiefs and leather thongs tied around the neck, canvas boots or rope-soled espadrilles were de rigueur.'

Jane Mulvagh

Boho, short for Bohemian, describes a free-spirited attitude and independent mind expressed through loose flowing clothes in natural fabrics such as linen and cotton. From the French for 'gypsy', the Boho style of embroidered tunics worn over floaty floral skirts, wide leather *faux*-coin belts with fur gilets thrown over the top and sheepskin boots, suits the 'gypsy' existence of today's girls at music festivals. Designer Isabel Marant has moved the look up a notch for the opening decade of the 21st century, moving away from the hand-crafted to create an 'Haute Bohemia' style. She shows striped micro-minis and black jackets, striped Lurex, tie-dyes mixed up with craft embellishments, suede boots with fringing, hot pink feathered earrings and chainmail scarves.

Boho also has a luxurious look for jet-setters on the move, created by Diane von Furstenberg's mini-kaftans, embellished peasant blouses, and sprigged florals worn with feathered headdresses. Marni create an individual look redolent of a free spirit with fluid layers in cotton, linen and silk in tawny brown colours with shirt dresses over striped leggings and printed head scarves knotted over casually done hair. For the evening jewels can be added in the shape of a little sequin or crystal embellishment and plenty of oversized petal-drop earrings made in horn with crystal and wooden resin bangles.

Top left and right: Tutti Frutti necklace and bracelet by Cartier, 1936.
Top centre: Feather brooch by Cassandra Goad.
Above: Isabel Marant, spring/summer 2010.

Sienna Miller (1981–)

Top left and right: Bee necklace and Peacock bracelet by Alex Monroe.
Centre left: Fern leaf brooch with diamonds by Hemmerle.
Centre right: Alhambra necklace by Van Cleef & Arpels.
Above: Sienna Miller, 2005.

In 2007 Sienna Miller launched her Twenty8Twelve fashion label with elder sister Savannah, featuring elements of Miller's own personal folksy Boho styling. She describes a Bohemian as 'someone who has the ability to appreciate beauty on a deep level, is a profound romantic who doesn't know any limits, whose world is their own creation, rather than living in a box'. Boho largely became fashionable when Sienna was photographed at Glastonbury music festival wearing floral smock tops, footless tights tucked into cowboy boots and a trilby hat. She accessorised her short skirts, leggings and oversized sunglasses with tangled golden bumblebee necklaces by Alex Monroe. Monroe also designs whimsical intricate filigree butterflies, birds, peacock feathers, apple lockets and charm bracelets hanging with fruits, pea pods, aubergines and watering cans which appeal to the Boho look's earthy nature. For a Boho-in-Ibiza look Sienna's evening looks are bright butterfly-hem Matthew Williamson dresses, flirty swing dresses and kaftans with sequins, with a glimmer of an H. Stern *Love Knot* diamond earring.

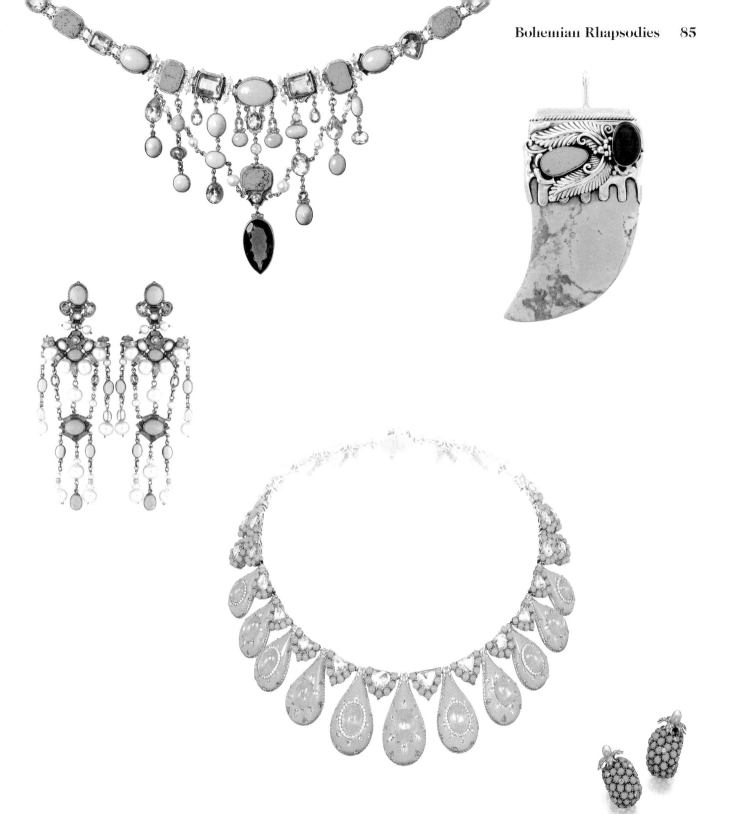

Turquoise

This blue-green ancient gemstone is an important part of Tibetan dress, which is attractive to the Boho crowd who appreciate the association with Buddhism. Early cultures thought that turquoise changed colour if the wearer was unwell, and the stone is still believed to have powerful talismanic properties. Today the sky-blue stone shines from Van Cleef & Arpels *Alhambra* collection in long loose chains to create a modern free-spirited Boho look. Simon Wilson at Butler & Wilson uses chunky turquoise cabochons and roughly hewn beads, in the style of the Navajo Indians in North America, for rings, belt buckles, cross pendants and cuffs.

Top left: Turquoise, amethyst and blue topaz, necklace with pearls and seed pearls on vermeil by Diego Percossi Papi.
Top right: Turquoise pendant by Butler & Wilson.
Centre left: 22ct yellow gold vermeil, turquoise peridot and freshwater pearl earrings by Diego Percossi Papi.
Centre right: Turquoise necklace by Chopard.
Above: Turquoise, cultured pearl and diamond earclips by Schlumberger for Tiffany, 1960s.

Maharani Style

The Maharani look began first appeared during the 1930s when Hindu princes and maharajahs flocked to Cartier to have chests of traditional Indian stones set into Western-style pieces. Europeans were so entranced with their exotic look that they began to commission Indian-style jewellery. For this market Cartier created the *Tutti Frutti* collection: rubies and emeralds in leaf-shaped cabochons, smooth ribbed beads, briolette diamonds, Jaipur enamels and Kashmir sapphires set into jewels, re-interpreting Indian motifs. During the 1960s travellers returning from the hippy trail brought back ethnic-style clothes such as Nehru jackets, flowing kaftans and loose djellabas which gradually became part of mainstream fashion as flower power exploded. Bohemian, Syrian-born Thea Porter turned the look into Maharani Exoticism, creating kaftans in rich silks, brocades, velvets and floaty chiffons with a touch of ancient civilisation. Highly embellished with Indian beading and sequin embroidery and decorated with braids and spangly trimmings she dressed the *beau monde* of the 1960s.

During the 16th century maharajahs brought artisans from around India to build magnificent decorative art showcases in Jaipur. Ever since then the city has been famed for its talented stone-cutting techniques. Marie-Hélène de Taillac spends seven months of the year in Jaipur creating simply constructed pieces in collaboration with the Gem Palace: 'I find it so inspirational to work at the source and they have incredible facilities for finding rough stone'. Inspired by the abstract colour mix of Emilio Pucci she fashions semi-precious stones into briolettes, traditionally a technique reserved for diamonds. Orange fire opals, lavender iolites, yellow citrines, peridots and pink tourmalines sparkle in the sunshine, hanging from wavy gold collars fit for a maharani.

Top left: Earrings by Dior.
Top centre: 18ct yellow gold earrings with rose-cut and round brilliant diamonds, square emeralds and square sapphires by Moussaieff.
Top right: Wave necklace by Marie-Hélène de Taillac.
Above: Earrings by Boucheron; necklace by the Gem Palace.

On the Red Carpet

'When is a girl going to wear a tiara if not at the Oscars?'

Salma Hayek, 1996

Actress Mary Pickford has been credited for linking the annual Academy Awards ceremony with the visual red-carpet extravaganza of couture dresses and jewels. Appealing to the public's love of Hollywood glamour she collected the Best Actress statuette in 1930 wearing a silk chiffon dress and arms full of diamonds. In the early days of the Awards Edith Head, Paramount studios' dress designer, created dresses that would portray the star in the image desired by the studio. Today's movie stars use their favourite designer or they hire a stylist to create the entire look. For example at the 2002 Oscars L'Wren Scott dressed Nicole Kidman in a pink pastel ruffled Chanel couture gown and commissioned Bulgari to create a matching necklace of 241 rare rough-cut pink diamonds.

Oscar styles can define the fashions of each decade from the silk taffeta ballgown and demure pearls worn by Olivia de Haviland in the 1940s to the elegance of Grace Kelly's champagne-coloured dress and elbow-length white gloves in the 1950s. Julie Christie accepted Best Actress for the film *Darling* wearing a 1960s-style metallic shiny gold pantsuit by Dan Bessant with disco-shaped golden hooped earrings. Cher captured the mood of extravagance in the 1980s with a two-foot plumed headdress and bare-midriff dress designed by Bob Mackie. The Academy almost cancelled the 75th diamond anniversary ceremony when the Iraq war broke out. But in the end it went ahead in dressed-down mode with minimal jewels: 'Celebrities suddenly demanded the choice of solemn black outfits and "compassionate" cocktail dresses', wrote *Vogue*.

Where actresses once led the world in experimentation and grand jewellery expressions today's stars have become more fearful of making a fashion faux pas, which has led to a parade of tasteful Oscar winners in off-the-shoulder sheath gowns accessorised with discreet jewels. 'It's become too stereotyped', says Caroline Scheufele, co-president of Chopard, who have dressed seven Best Actress winners in elegant diamond earrings in the first decade of the new century, 'I wish they would be more out-going and adventurous with their fashion and jewels'.

Top left: Tiara ring by Chaumet.
Centre: Tiara by Chaumet.
Top right: Necklace by Autore.
Above: Carey Mulligan at the 82nd Academy Awards, 2010.

Top right: Diamond Wreath necklace by Harry Winston.
Above left: Diamond drop earrings by Harry Winston.
Above right: The Hope Diamond.
Above: Madonna wearing Harry Winston at the Oscars.

Harry Winston (1896–1978)

For the 1944 Academy Awards the famous Fifth Avenue jeweller Harry Winston loaned the actress Jennifer Jones a diamond necklace to wear when collecting her Best Actress statuette for *Song of Bernadette*. This began the trend of 'diamond loaning' with each nominated actress receiving a hand-written note from Ronald, Harry Winston's son, congratulating them and inviting them to view the new collection. It is acknowledged that the tuxedo-wearing Harry Winston guards have walked the Oscar red carpet more times than any leading actor. At one point Winston owned a third of the world's most famous diamonds, creating a 'Court of Jewels', including the blue Hope Diamond, which toured major American cities during the 1950s. Winston's iconic design was the diamond *Wreath* necklace, inspired by traditional holiday wreaths, made with 128 brilliant, frosted 'holly leaf' diamond cuts. 'If I could', Winston said, 'I would attach diamonds directly onto a woman's skin'.

Elizabeth Taylor (1932–)

Wearing a low-cut violet gown by Edith Head with the spectacular 69.72-carat Taylor–Burton diamond flashing at her décolletage Elizabeth Taylor was the epitome of Oscar glamour in 1969. 'This diamond', declared Richard Burton, 'has so many carats it's almost a turnip'. By contrast, however, at her first appearance in 1949 aged just 17 Taylor wore a demure ballgown strewn with forget-me-nots with a simple strand of pearls. Taylor suffers a well-documented addiction to diamonds ensuring, unlike other actresses, that she always wore her own jewels, whether a magnificent suite of emeralds and diamonds by Bulgari or a yellow-and-white diamond daisy parure by Van Cleef & Arpels with brilliant green chrysophrase leaves. When her husband, Mike Todd, won an Oscar in 1956 for *Around the World in 80 Days* Taylor wore a tiara to the awards ceremony. 'It wasn't fashionable to wear a tiara then', she said, 'but I wore it anyway because he was my king'.

Above: Elizabeth Taylor wears the Taylor-Burton diamond at the Oscar Ball in Beverly Hills, 1970.
Below left and right: Earrings and necklace by Chopard.
Bottom left: Necklace by Bulgari.
Bottom right: Les Incroyables earrings by Dior.

Vogue

CHRISTMAS
NUMBER

NOVEMBER 1935

'We, *the couturiers, can no longer live without
the cinema anymore than the cinema can live
without us. We corroborate each other's instinct.*'
Lucien Lelong

Allure of the Sirens

American cinema in the 1930s was a popular form of escapism during the Depression both in the US and in Europe. Movie stars had a huge influence on women around the world who wanted copies of the glamorous fashion and jewellery they saw on screen. The siren look was epitomised by two stars, Marlene Dietrich and Katharine Hepburn, who were dressed by Madeleine Vionnet in sensual crepe-de-chine and satin bias-cut draped designs. 'Designers make dresses, artists make dreams', said Vionnet, whose body-hugging look was based on the Greek *peplos*, a rectangular sheet draped around the body.

For cinematographers working in black and white, jewels were important accessories, as they could create dramatic glints of light. Maura Spiegel explains in *The Nature of Diamonds*: 'For the shallow close-up shot of a star bedecked in diamonds time almost stopped, as the camera seemed to absorb the luminescence'. Siren jewels were imaginative and bold, constructed into diamond-set pleats, spirals scrolls and plaques, which echoed the architectural detail of the grand new cinemas. Katharine Hepburn wore a large diamond 'bicycle' clip which held up her train while dancing; and Marlene Dietrich's 128-carat emerald cabochon, 'the size of a bantam's egg' according to *Vogue*, was arranged to slip between the prongs of a ring or on to the clasp of a wide diamond bracelet. This period saw the invention of the earring clip—a faster solution than previously awkward screw fittings—in triangular, platinum scroll- and fan-shaped motifs which covered the whole earlobe. More recent siren looks appeared in the 1960s at Biba who revived the 1930s' cinematic style with their graphic black and gold décor; and contemporary evening gowns by Donna Karan swing with fluid drape effects redolent of the sensuality of the screen siren's silhouette.

Top left: Platinum single clip set with brilliant- and baguette-cut diamonds by Cartier, c. 1938.
Top right: Platinum clip of mitre-shape-set amethysts and diamonds by Boucheron, c. 1940.
Above: Donna Karan, spring 2009.

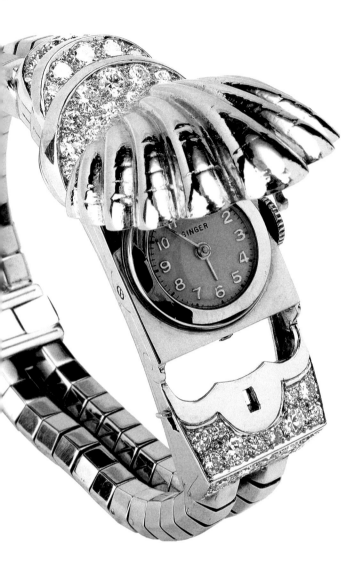

Mae West (1893–1980)

Top left: 14ct gold and diamond bracelet watch by Paul Flato, c. 1938–40.
Top right: Watch by Van Cleef & Arpels.
Centre: Necklace by Graff.
Above: Mae West, c. 1936.

The classic siren cut of 1930s' slinky dresses did not suit Mae West's feminine curves, the inspiration for Schiaparelli's *Shocking* hourglass-shaped scent bottle. So instead she dressed like a Belle Époque *grande dame* in heavy-boned corsets, oversized picture hats, elaborate coiffures and floor-length gowns with sequined fishtail hems. 'Say what you like about long dresses but they cover a multitude of shins', she wise-cracked. She seldom appeared on screen or in public without parading her eye-catching diamonds, her every finger covered in what she termed her 'daytime diamonds'. Her comment 'No gold digging for me! I take diamonds. We may be off the gold standard some day', showed that Mae was no dumb blonde, but a woman investing wisely in her future financial security. In the 1933 movie *She Done Him Wrong* West played Lady 'Diamond' Lou, famous for her beauty and the diamonds her many beaux had given her. 'A gifted diamond shines so much better than one you buy yourself', she commented, summing up an era when movie stars amassed serious fine jewellery collections through gifts from ardent suitors.

Suzanne Belperron (1900–83)

In tune with 1930s' sensuous elegance Suzanne Belperron eschewed dainty white diamond and platinum antique-inspired pieces in favour of over-sized, curvy organic creations. Dressed all in black with long painted red fingernails she received Hollywood stars such as Gary Cooper, Fred Astaire and Charlie Chaplin, who flocked to her tiny Parisian shop for the jewellery equivalent of a couture fitting. Her avant-garde creations feature flower blossoms in chalcedony with articulated petals, bunches of grapes, ferns, conch shells and large pine cones bulging with semi-precious stones. Belperron pioneered the technique of sinking gemstones into rock crystal and quartz to create a dramatic new style.

Above: Marlene Dietrich, 1935.
Below: Grey gold, nickel-plated steel and diamond bangle by Belperron, 1934.
Bottom left: Sapphire and ruby brooch by Belperron, 1950s.
Bottom right: Rock crystal and diamond bangle–bracelet by Herz-Belperron.

Pretty in Pastels

'Front row in the Paris couture shows and the chit-chat seems to be as frothy as the creations on the catwalk — clouds of cream puffery and rose-tinted tulle, petals of embroidered silk and trails of pale lace.'

Justine Picardie

An era when debutantes danced the night away displaying their girly innocence in ballrooms full of shimmering evening dresses, the 1950s defined femininity through pastel colours. Norman Hartnell and Hardy Amies whipped up frothy gowns in blue grosgrain, powder-pink duchesse satin, or lavender silk taffeta. Trimmed with broderie-anglaise roses and bows worked in silver thread over layers of netting these airy sugary concoctions were light as a meringue. The jewelled frosting was added mainly by opalescent pearls and delicate baby-blue-coloured aquamarines set into brooches and dress clips with a sprinkling of inherited diamond icing. As fashion magazines began to colour-coordinate fabrics with make-up, Max Factor introduced a new lipstick called *Strawberry Meringue*, and titanium was added to bright lipstick to tone them down so they resembled peaches-and-cream or pearly pink pastel sticks.

Recently pastels have been used to show the softer side of fashion. Christopher Kane uses scallop-edged nude sheaths to create a matte base for a pale shade. Michael Kors is awash with sea-foam blues, mint greens and washed-out lavender hues with flesh-tone tulle-edged cocktail dresses which he showed with large, clear Lucite-faceted ball necklaces and sleek cuffs designed by Alexis Bittar. Soft blue, mint, lilac and lemon cocktail dresses by Christopher Bailey are shown with brown leather belts and chunky sculpted cuffs in checked acrylic. He sweetened the look of the classic Burberry trench with sherbet-shaded hues and ruched sleeves. Pastel fashions conjure up soft fruit sorbets and ice-cream colour palettes, and although jewels should enhance the paleness and delicacy of the clothes they need a modern edge to lessen the sugar-spun style. A discreet glimmer of a moonstone set into a wide white gold cuff by Ritz Fine Jewellery, watery drops of chalcedony hanging from an earring or long flowing chains set with iridescent pale lemon yellow citrines and aquamarines by Moussaieff give a gentle glint of colour without dominating. Designer Tom McEwan makes contemporary cocktail rings with a big flash of stone set into a twirling metal nest for sea-green beryls, blush-pink quartz and powder-blue topaz which gives the pastel statement a fresh twist with some feminine energy. Pomellato's Italian Capri and Luna collections shine with translucent light blue, dusty pink and chalcedony hues set together with rock crystal in delicate clouds to emphasise their lightness.

Top left: Necklace by Chopard.
Above: Capri rings by Pomellato.
Pink diamond cuff by Chopard.

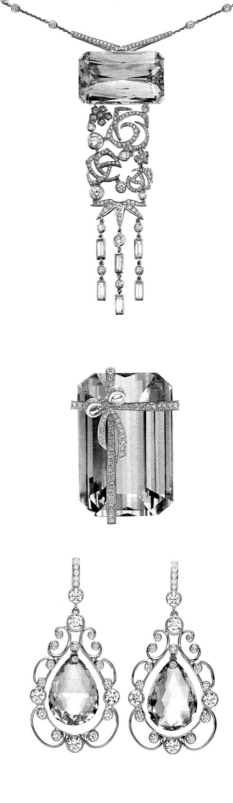

Top left: Kunzite necklace
by Paloma Picasso.
Top right: Pink diamond necklace
by Boodles.
Centre right: Tiffany kunzite Bow
brooch with diamonds set in platinum.
Above right: Morganite drop earrings
with diamonds set in 18ct rose gold
by Tiffany & Co.
Above: Morganite cuff by Boodles.

American Pinks

Kunzite is the colour of a dusty pink Cadillac on the San Diego roads, the area where
the stone was originally found. Known for its lustrous rosy lilac-pink shade, the stone
was named after jewellery king-pin George Frederick Kunz, the world's most famous
gemologist, who worked at Tiffany from 1880 until 1927. It is called the 'evening stone'
because of its phosphorescence which softly glows in low light. A few years after the
discovery of kunzite in 1903 another pink gemstone was identified, found in California,
Brazil, Madagascar and Afghanistan. Kunz named it morganite after the famous
US industrialist John Pierpont Morgan who was an extensive collector of gemstones.
Morganite can have a deeper more saturated purplish pink than kunzite, which can
lose colour in intense light, giving it a faded, washed-out but perfect pastel appeal.

Shaun Leane (1969–)

Famed for his darkly romantic jewels and creations for Alexander McQueen's catwalk shows, Shaun Leane also imbues some collections with a light touch and colour. Leane's *White Light* is a masterpiece: it uses 2,477 Forevermark Diamonds set into delicate icicle-style white gold and diamond collets surrounded by pavé-set diamond branches with shimmering leaves in opalescent enamel, with a hint of grey-blue early morning frost. His *Cherry Blossom* collection perfectly hits the nearly-nude to creamy-apricot silhouettes on the runways with pale pink enamelled flowers, and tiny pink pearls sitting on delicate oxidised silver and gold branches which wrap around earlobes and fingers. Leane was inspired by the Japanese legend that cherry blossom seeds are sprinkled by a goddess from the clouds of Mount Fuji. The rings show each stage of the flower opening from bud to full springtime blossom.

Above: Shaun Leane and Erin O'Connor attend the launch party of White Light crafted for Forevermark, 22 April 2009, London.
Below left: Cherry Blossom collection by Shaun Leane.
Below right: White Light by Shaun Leane in collaboration with Steinmetz for the Forevermark Precious collection.

Dior's New Look

'I designed clothes for flower-like women, with rounded shoulders, full feminine busts and hand-span waists above enormous spreading skirts.'

Christian Dior

The post-war look of padded shoulders, short hemlines and boxy jackets was too reminiscent of uniforms for Christian Dior, so he decided to create a new silhouette inspired by the femininity of Parisian women. This started what *Vogue* termed a 'revolution in fashion', creating the ultimate hourglass figure with wasp waists whipped in by corsetry and girdles above yards of opulent fabric swirling to the ankles. Initially the New Look's extravagant use of fabric — 25 yards for a short cocktail frock — caused controversy after the parsimonious era of clothing coupons. King George V forbade the young princesses, Elizabeth and Margaret, from wearing the style, fearing it might set a bad example at a time when rationing was still in force. But Dior was unrepentant: 'War has passed out of sight', he responded. 'What did the weight of my sumptuous materials, my heavy velvets and brocades, matter? When hearts were light mere fabrics could not weigh the body down'.

Having lived through the Belle Époque Dior liked to add 19th-century touches such as fringed bows and fabric knots to his stiff taffeta, satin and wool dresses. And following suit jewellers began to mimic the femininity of his full ballerina skirts with their delicate fringes, bows, knots and loops in mesh and plaited gold work. Encouraged by the spring of a new age jewellery designers made a myriad of precious-set flower sprays, leaves, ferns and feathered necklaces to embellish the low necklines of the New Look. Inspired by a vintage backstage photograph of Dior hurriedly dressing his models, John Galliano at Dior staged a 2009 couture show, *Fever in the Cabine*, which presented the clothes in the chic dove grey Dior Paris salon exactly as they would have been shown in the 1950s. Galliano has reworked the New Look for the 21st century in a collection of basques, girdles, lace-trimmed slips and vintage-style black bras, teaming wasp-waisted garments with fluorescent lilac, orange and lime wide-collared peplum jackets, satin tulip-shaped skirts and padded hip coats.

Top left: Textured gold bird brooch
set with bi-colour tourmaline and
diamonds by Sterlé c. 1960.
Top right: Aquamarine and diamond
brooch by Sterlé, 1950s.
Centre: Malachite, mother-of-pearl
and diamond bird brooch by Sterlé,
c. 1960.
Above: Coral and diamond brooch
by Sterlé, 1950s.

Pierre Sterlé (1905–78)

Following World War II master jeweller Pierre Sterlé created revolutionary jewellery
designs featuring overlapping twisted leaves, feathers, ribbons, and birds. Sterlé's
feminine pieces, which well suited the wide lily-like skirts of the New Look, emerged
as a result of his collaborations with the best couturiers in Paris at the time such
as Dior, Balmain and Jacques Fath. Sterlé was inspired by the heavy and opulent
fabrics of the New Look — velvets, rich brocade, stiff taffeta and duchesse satin.
He manipulated gold into opulent fabric-like textures such as rich gold fringes, cord,
basket-weave and his famous 'angel-wire' mesh. Bringing a great sense of movement
into his jewellery, he looped this gold chain-knit mesh into the plumage of a bird's
wing on malachite, coral or amethyst bodies, with delicate diamonds mounted lightly
on a draping 'feathered' tail.

Van Cleef & Arpels

Van Cleef & Arpels had patented their 'mystery setting' — a unique method of mounting stones as if they are floating in air with no visible signs of metal — in 1934, but the technique was perfected in the more complex spirals and curves of 1950s' jewellery. The setting uses delicate spiders-webs of gossamer-light gold and platinum threads into which the stones are placed, so they seem to flow like an uninterrupted river of colour over the stones' rounded forms. As a result precious stones could be used in a more supple way and adapted to any three-dimensional form to bring a colourful depth to a petal or the plumage of a bird. Van Cleef & Arpels' *Boule* rings and *Ruban* bracelets were set with perfectly matched carpets of verdant emeralds, sapphires and pigeons-blood rubies like elegant ribbons of colour. These jewels quickly became the sought-after accessory for sophisticated fashionistas such as the Duchess of Windsor who pinned leafy-looking mystery-set clips to the collars of their New Look suits.

Above and below: Diamonds and rubies in Van Cleef & Arpels' 'mystery setting'.

Punks, Piercings and Pins

'Punk wasn't class-based: the working-class kid and the privileged rebel walked down the King's Road in mini tartan kilts, leggings and torn PVC, rubber, leather and dustbin liners.'

Jane Mulvagh

In the early 1980s 16-year-old Elizabeth Hurley joined the punk-rock scene sporting pink hair and a nose-ring. Years later in 1994 she reprised the style when she wore a black ripped Versace dress held together with safety pins at the premiere of the film *Four Weddings and a Funeral*. It is a style that has never gone away.

Punk began as an anti-fashion urban street culture closely aligned to a music movement epitomised by bands like The Ramones and Malcolm McLaren's Sex Pistols. As a style punk explored the possibilities of decay and challenged the concept of clothes as a means to beautify the individual by deconstructing them: edges were frayed, trousers intentionally torn to reveal laddered tights, fabrics destroyed and defaced by anarchic messages and anti-establishment motifs often featuring an image of Queen Elizabeth II. The garments would then be refashioned in a crude manner using safety pins à la Hurley. The look was aggressively accessorised with heavy Doc Marten boots, zips, spiked dog collars, neck chains made from padlocks, and razor-blade earrings or pendants. During the 1970s Zandra Rhodes used elements of refined punk style in her collections featuring gold safety pins and chains to join uneven hems.

Tough styling appeared on this century's catwalks by Charles Anastase who showed purple denim skinny legs encased in platform boots with rivets, and defaced biker jackets with blanket skirts made of tartan. Jean-Paul Gaultier struck a rebellious chord with tartan skirts, PVC, metal studs and fishnet tights. Jeweller Ileana Makri chose the safety pin as a utilitarian object that she could transform into an object of beauty for her contemporary collection, creating safety pins with coloured diamonds and ruby-encrusted heads curved into rings or on fine chain pendants.

Top: Pin by Belmacz.
Above: Elizabeth Hurley wears Gianni Versace, 1994.

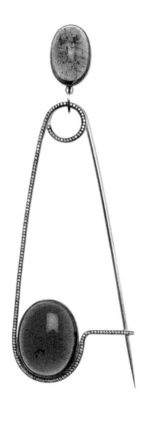

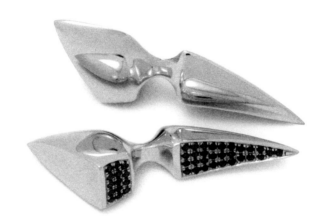

Top left: Green amethyst and 18ct pink gold ring by Ileana Makri (part of the Makri/Marios Schwab collection). **Top centre and right:** Jewellery from Ileana Makri's Safety Pin collection. **Centre:** Black diamond Spur cufflinks by Hannah Martin. **Below:** Vivienne Westwood, 2010.

Vivienne Westwood (1941–)

Punk's London HQ during the 1970s was the King's Road shop Let it Rock opened by Vivienne Westwood's partner, Malcolm McLaren, and where she sold her avant-garde designs in zippered leather. Now a *grande dame* of fashion, Westwood has kept her cutting-edge punk sensibility combining it with the best of British tailoring, historic French chic, and bondage references wrapped into bustled dresses. She injects frayed Scottish tartan capes flung across one shoulder with clashing designs, challenging her fashion audience with political slogans like 'We need an estimated $30 billion per year to save the rain forest' splashed punk-style on a T-shirt. Always creatively confrontational Westwood cycles around London wearing a 19th-century Italian coral tiara decorated with oak leaves and acorns. Although now at the heart of the establishment it was reported that Dame Vivienne collected her OBE from the Queen, in defiant punk style — wearing no knickers.

Postmodern Punk

Female punks rejected conventional ideas of prettiness, making their jewellery out of threatening spiked bands, studded with safety pins. Everyday objects were used to make shocking statements such as bin-bag dresses and razor-blade jewels. *Vogue* seemed unwittingly to report this future trend in December 1921, writing: 'When every least member of the anatomy is hung with diamonds (omitting only the nose ring) it is still possible to add to one's glory by carrying a jewelled vanity-case ….' Their punk granddaughters added to their glory with piercings for nose, cheeks, tongue, navel and lip. Punk-style jewels have become mainstream fashion accessories, softened by the 21st-century designer's use of precious stones. Jade Jagger made diamond-set revolver pendants for Garrard. Hannah Martin makes hard-edged androgynous gold *Spur* and *Spike* rings as well as threatening *Knuckleduster* rings spread over three fingers. Her chunky claw-shaped rings are fierce looking but, set with brilliant-cut rubies and black diamonds, they have a glamorous and sophisticated edge. New-wave jeweller Dominic Jones, with Alice Dellal, has a punk chic aesthetic visible in his *Tooth and Nail* collection, with spiky yellow gold stem necklaces, rose-gold claws set with rubies and black gold with sapphires.

Above: Spur ring with rubies by Hannah Martin.
Below left: Stud ring by Hannah Martin.
Below right: Pearl clasp necklace with pavé by Hannah Martin.
Bottom: Jewellery by Dominic Jones.

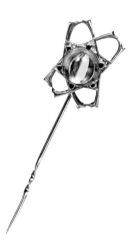

The Dandy

*'The Duke of Windsor had style…
in every buckle on his kilt, every check
of his country suit.'*

Diana Vreeland

The term 'dandy' was first used before the American Revolution in the song *Yankee Doodle*, whose lyrics conveyed the sentiment that a pony and a few feathers would turn a poor American into a sophisticated and stylish European. During the 18th century the word came to describe modish young English aristocrats who wore layers of lace ruffles, knee buckles, gold embroidery and foot-high powdered wigs. They typically carried decorative accessories such as walking sticks, ornate snuff boxes and swords with diamond handles. The dandys' role model was 'Beau' Brummell, whose chief claim to fame was his friendship with the Prince Regent, the future King George IV. His style incorporated tailored dark blue tailcoats, white shirts with large cravats and pantaloons tucked into riding boots.

Ever since, modern dandies have taken their sartorial lead from Britain. During the 1930s Hollywood celebrities such as Fred Astaire and Gary Cooper travelled to tailors Anderson & Sheppard on Savile Row in search of the 'London Look'. Fred Astaire took his tailored blazers and slacks back to Los Angeles: there he wore them with bright blue socks, perfectly tied cravats and a brightly patterned tie looped through his trousers as a belt. A classic Cartier Tank watch, gold signet ring and discreet gold chain-link identity bracelet were his everyday jewels. When dressing up in Astaire's iconic look of 'white tie and tails' dandies wear onyx and diamond vintage dress studs and cufflinks with an elegant dress watch such as Chaumet's appropriately named *Dandy*. Designer and film director Tom Ford, who cuts a dash in his chic black or burgundy velvet tuxedos, has updated the British look, designing with playful 'ducal' patterns, loud Prince of Wales checks and paisley shirts worn with oversized velour bow ties. Ford creates 18th-century-style 18-carat-gold-dipped walking sticks; and rapper Andre 3000, who also subverts the English country look with his hot pink checks, green plaid plus fours and flat caps, tucks his trousers into Brummell-style polished boots.

Top left: Cufflinks by Chaumet.
Centre left: Tie-pin by David Webdale.
Centre right: Ruby- and diamond-set pendant watch, 1905.
Above: Fred Astaire in white tie and tails, 1936.

The Duke of Windsor (1894–1972)

A prerequisite for a dandy is a good tailor, and Frederick Scholte of Savile Row provided that service for the Duke of Windsor who, in the 1920s and 1930s, was considered the best-dressed man in the world. Both dashing and conservative the Duke created trends for double-breasted jackets with long roll lapels, navy-blue Guards' overcoats and the Windsor knotted tie. Following World War I the Duke was the first man to wear a white waistcoat with a black dinner jacket. He often wore full Highland regalia: his kilts were made in the Balmoral tartan reserved for use by the royal family or the Royal Stewart in bright scarlet, green and yellow tartan mixed with black-and-white hounds-tooth jackets; the Duchess, on the other hand, had her kilts made by Dior in Paris. The Duke supported traditional Scottish industries by wearing local tweeds dyed in the colours of bracken and heather, with colourful patterned Fair Isle sweaters. 'I believe in bright colours for sportsmen', he wrote, 'the louder they are the better I like them'. The Duke amassed a large collection of royal tie-pins which he had dismounted during the 1930s, setting the jewelled heads (such as a diamond-framed medallion of his parents George V and Queen Mary) in gold basket-weave handbags, notebook holders and cigarette cases as gifts for his wife.

Above: Edward, Prince of Wales at Le Bourget airport, Paris, 1931.
Below left and bottom right: Vintage cufflinks at SJ Phillips.
Below right: Engraved cigarette case by Cartier.
Bottom left: Tiger decor prestige fountain pen by Cartier.

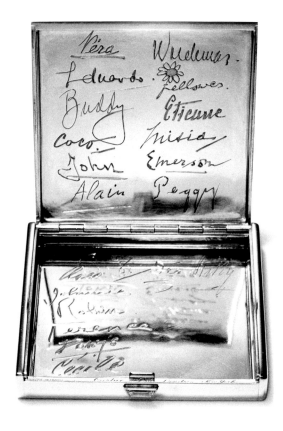

Fob Watches

Pocket watches were developed during the 16th century, and soon became required equipment for railroad workers during the latter part of the 19th century to enable them to keep accurate time, until they were superseded by wristwatches which officers during World War I found much easier for timekeeping. In 1939 Cartier was commissioned by the Duchess of Windsor to make a gold pocket watch for her husband with a compass on the reverse side. It was engraved with the words, 'No excuses for going in the wrong direction'. Fob watch fashion is kept alive by movies stars such as Steve McQueen, who wore one during the filming of *The Thomas Crown Affair*; Jude Law as dapper Dr Watson in the 2009 film *Sherlock Holmes* also sparked a revival for classic Victorian styles. Richard Mille creates an edgy, modern tourbillon version of the fob watch in US airforce jet carbon nanofibre with titanium chains. Ralph Lauren recreates an aristocratic English dandy look using heavy-linked gold chains, known as a 'fob', attached to a pocket watch visible across an immaculately cut waistcoat.

Top left and centre: Fob watches by Ernest Jones.
Top right: Extra flat pocket watch by Cartier Paris, 1905.

'*The model he imagines is, first and foremost, a beautiful object, excellently made and finely sewn; so that if, years afterwards, it were discovered at the back of some cupboard, although the fashion which inspired it has long gone out of date, it would still inspire astonishment.*'

Cecil Beaton

Haute Couture

The 'golden hands' who painstakingly craft high jewellery creations follow the same precise traditions as couture seamstresses and embroiderers, displaying the heritage of what the French craft culture calls their *savoir-faire*. Both arts share a passion for materials: the couturier for duchesse satin, fine organdie and lace; the jeweller for brushed gold, tassels of rubies and ribbons of diamonds. This similarity of craftsmanship led the Fédération Française de la Couture, the body that maintains the grandeur and exclusivity of haute couture, to include Parisian fine jewellers on the agenda during Paris Fashion Week in 2010. The production of couture was based on a division of labour, which Claire Wilcox describes in *The Golden Age of Couture* as: 'Separate in-house workshops for dressmaking (*flou*) and tailoring (*tailleur*) supported by a luxury trade in trimmings and accessories supplied by specialist ateliers all over France'.

At the zenith of couture working during the 1950s six weeks was the lead time for a couture collection. Now it takes twelve days, with fifteen to twenty girls working on one dress. Today the materials used have become more adventurous: for example boiled and painted mussel shells were hand sewn onto fur for Christian Lacroix; and a realistic beaded panther for Jean-Paul Gaultier took 2,500 hours to complete. The Maison Lesage embroidered a black silk organza dress for Chanel's autumn / winter 1996 collection. The application of thousands of black, gold and red sequins and bronze seed beads in Chinoiserie motifs in the style of the Coromandel screens in Coco Chanel's collection took over 900 hours to complete. It has taken Shaun Leane four years to complete a white gold chainmail full-length glove with pavé-set diamond fingernails and knuckle hinges decorated with flying diamond birds of peace for socialite Daphne Guinness. As a toile is made in linen or muslin for a couture gown, which can be manipulated, marked and adapted during fittings before being created in an exclusive fabric, Shaun Leane created a brass toile for the glove, which was adapted to fit Guinness's arm. The same spirit and craftsmanship of 1950s' haute couture is evident today in prêt-à-porter collections as more and more fashion houses such as Hermès, Armani Privé, Gucci, Louis Vuitton and Versace demonstrate design, imagination and handwork at its most exquisitely beautiful in both fashion and fine jewels.

Top: Midnight Pumpkin brooch in yellow and white diamonds and platinum by Michelle Ong.
Above: Detail of Coromandel coat by Chanel.

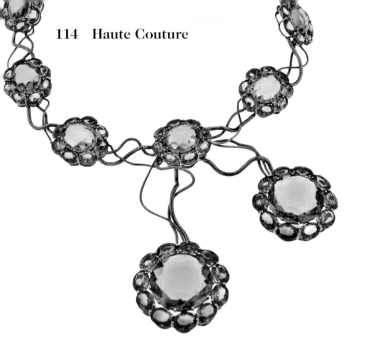

Hubert (1927–) *and James de Givenchy* (1963–)

Hubert de Givenchy, who always worked in a white lab coat, was a couturier who brought French style to American fashion. His mantra of 'keep it simple' eliminated everything that interfered with the line of the garment. 'The dress must follow the body of a woman, not the body follow the shape of a dress', he said. The quintessential Givenchy always-perfectly-dressed style was epitomised by Jacqueline Kennedy, who famously wore Givenchy at her husband's funeral in 1963, and by Audrey Hepburn whom he dressed both on and off the screen. As Holly Golightly, in *Breakfast at Tiffany's* Audrey wore Givenchy's ultimate Little Black Dress with ropes of pearls which has become a cult image for both fashion and jewellery.

The Givenchy tradition continues in Hubert's nephew, James de Givenchy, who learned what couture could do for a woman while watching his uncle fitting models. James channels this legacy of elegance and charm into stylish jewellery such as armbands of amethysts studded with turquoise buttons or a Mexican fire opal and diamond Nautilus brooch. He creates breathtaking colour combinations, such as deep papal purple amethyst set into red lacquer; his pieces have a delicacy from every angle. 'I think I'm like my uncle — his couture was easily recognised from the finishing touches', he says.

Top left: Peridot, blue sapphire and 18ct yellow gold flower necklace by James de Givenchy, Taffin.
Top right: Mandarin garnet, pink sapphire, old-mine diamond, coral and 18ct yellow gold flower brooch by James de Givenchy, Taffin.
Centre: Emerald-cut beryl, demantoid garnet and 18ct yellow gold bracelet by James de Givenchy, Taffin.
Above: Audrey Hepburn with Hubert de Givenchy, 1991.

Michelle Ong

Hong Kong jeweller Michelle Ong, who precociously bought her first diamond jewel as a teenager, conjures up her own style of East-meets-West in fluid green jade and sapphire dragons, succulent ruby-seeded pomegranates and clouds billowing with delicate diamonds. Using extraordinary stones in potent contrasting colours she designs through what she calls the idea of 'multiple echoes of the past and present coinciding'. Some pieces with large polished pink tourmalines, blackened areas or precious trapeze-like hoops resonate with a strength and dynamism, while others are as light as a puff of smoke. Like couturiers cutting their precious cloth Ong fashions diamonds into an antique lace-effect fabric which she works into magnificent Belle Époque-style chokers, shimmering brown diamond crochet-like collars and slithery slips of diamond-ribbon bracelets.

Above and below: All pieces by Michelle Ong.

The Rock Chick

'I wish I had invented blue jeans. They have expression. Modesty, sex appeal, simplicity — all that I hope for in my clothes.'

Yves Saint Laurent

The inspiration for today's wanna-be rock chicks is singer and actress Marianne Faithfull who created the original look — fur coats, feather boas, large-brimmed hats and over-sized sunglasses — on the arm of Rolling Stone Mick Jagger during the 1960s. The urban chic look for young rock chicks now features a top-heavy silhouette of sharply cut leather jackets, loose T-shirts with silver crystal beading, leather mini-dresses with inserted diagonal chains or skinny jeans topped off with a touch of vintage such as a trilby hat. Christophe Decarnin is the current designer of choice for rock chicks, who queue up for Balmain's ripped and embroidered jeans, black bustiers and leather blazers which display a touch of 1980s' glitter and excess. Gucci has created a luxy rock chick look with gold chains threaded through hipster jeans tucked into over-the-knee riding boots worn with chiffon print dresses and feathery fur jackets that Faithfull herself would have been proud of.

Top left: Bracelet by Ann Dexter Jones.
Top right: White gold Luna ring by Shaun Leane.
Above: The Midnight Hour watch in black onyx and gold by Ann Dexter Jones.

Gilt, glitter and diamante might have dominated in the past but rock chicks today keep it real, slinging diamonds through the loopholes of their jeans and wearing enamel and precious stone pieces with a touch of the sinister by Delfina Delettrez. Inspired by gothic stories and her Fendi grandmother's antique crucifix Delettrez makes edgy-looking frogs, skull rings and spider bracelets in iron, copper and gold, mixed with Tuscan marble, bone and wood with irreverently scattered precious stones. Her knuckledusters may have a hard-edged look but they are refined with precious stones and polished gold. Ileana Makri's three large sea-green amethysts span two fingers; and Georgina Chapman's chunky rings for Garrard are softly feathered with diamonds but keep the edgy rocker look with urban-styled blackened gold. With an anarchic spirit Diane von Furstenberg created her polished gold heavy-linked *Power* collection because she wanted to 'create rings for women that would knock men out'.

Jeans

Denim may be one of the world's oldest fabrics but it consistently appeals to youth culture. The name 'blue jean' is derived from *bleu de Gênes* [Genoa blue], the port whose sailors loved the fabric because it was so hard wearing. In 1885 Levi Strauss began creating jean dungarees for the mining communities in California. In the US the sex appeal of famous jeans wearers Elvis Presley, Marlon Brando and James Dean gave jeans a rock-and-roll chic during the 1950s, even leading some US schools to ban their pupils from wearing the fabric. Now blue jeans priced at £2,000 or more dominate the runways in Paris and leading designers often collaborate with jeans brands. Alber Elbaz linked Lanvin with the denim label Acne saying, 'When you think about it you can do anything with jeans — even jewellery'. Calvin Klein gave jeans a 'designer' tag in the 1980s as his brand of sexy jeans was advertised by Brooke Shields with the words, 'Nothing comes between me and my Calvin's'.

Above: Denim watch by Chopard.
Below left: Phoenix brooch by De Beers.
Below right: Feather Duster ring by Georgina Chapman for Garrard.
Bottom left: Eclipse Porcupine blue sapphire ring with black rhodium by Annoushka.
Bottom right: Flame ring with spinels, Fire of London collection by Stephen Webster for Garrard.

Go-to-Bed Jewels

Aware of the trend towards casual fashions during the 1970s Gianni Bulgari realised that diamond fashions too had to become less formal to remain relevant to a woman's wardrobe. As he explained to *Women's Wear Daily*: 'We want to do important things casually so they're not just worn for special occasions'. Bulgari's *Go-to-Bed-With* diamond jewellery, styled for free-flowing kaftans which could be worn all day long, still retained the company's Roman heritage and history of craftsmanship. Solange Azagury-Partridge creates diamond tattoos in the shapes of peace signs, zodiac symbols and spinning star rings for rock chicks: she describes them as as 'tatty diamonds to be worn all day with jeans'. Kate Moss keeps her dressed-down rock chick look by wearing one long elegant silver tusk-shaped earring, a tiny tusk hanging off a diamond set ring and a chunky onyx and diamond bracelet. Ann Dexter Jones wanted to make 'a rock-and-roll version of the ID bracelet' using lapis, emeralds, diamonds and heavy-linked macho straps. The hands of her watches are set permanently at midnight as befits all-night party girls.

Above: Kate Moss at Glastonbury music festival, 2005.
Below left: Bracelets by Bulgari.
Bottom left: Beaten silver bangles by Ram Rijal at Talisman Gallery, and antique tribal cuffs by Talisman Gallery.
Below right: Coral necklace by Bulgari.

Animal Prints

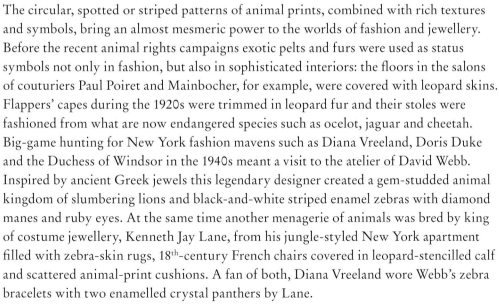

'I did panthers, tigers, lions, monkeys with all varieties of coloured beads in stripes and polka dots.'

Kenneth Jay Lane

The circular, spotted or striped patterns of animal prints, combined with rich textures and symbols, bring an almost mesmeric power to the worlds of fashion and jewellery. Before the recent animal rights campaigns exotic pelts and furs were used as status symbols not only in fashion, but also in sophisticated interiors: the floors in the salons of couturiers Paul Poiret and Mainbocher, for example, were covered with leopard skins. Flappers' capes during the 1920s were trimmed in leopard fur and their stoles were fashioned from what are now endangered species such as ocelot, jaguar and cheetah. Big-game hunting for New York fashion mavens such as Diana Vreeland, Doris Duke and the Duchess of Windsor in the 1940s meant a visit to the atelier of David Webb. Inspired by ancient Greek jewels this legendary designer created a gem-studded animal kingdom of slumbering lions and black-and-white striped enamel zebras with diamond manes and ruby eyes. At the same time another menagerie of animals was bred by king of costume jewellery, Kenneth Jay Lane, from his jungle-styled New York apartment filled with zebra-skin rugs, 18th-century French chairs covered in leopard-stencilled calf and scattered animal-print cushions. A fan of both, Diana Vreeland wore Webb's zebra bracelets with two enamelled crystal panthers by Lane.

Chopard co-president Caroline Scheufele created an *Animal World* for the company's 150th anniversary in 2010. But unlike the 1940s-style tame-looking creatures her contemporary zoo includes a frog holding a crown with a large yellow diamond, playful brown diamond monkeys jumping onto foliage-covered pendants and glistening ants: 'I even wanted to do ugly animals', she said. Modern fashion designers bring a fresh twist to the synergy of animal patterns: Roberto Cavalli makes abstract vibrant pink and green dyed animal print for patchwork skirts and billowing maxi dresses; while Dolce & Gabbana create optical illusions with large-scale leopard-print frilled shirts worn above a smaller print.

Top left: Leo bracelet by Roberto Coin.
Top centre: Rose gold Brazilian rainbow Boa design pavé-set diamond bangle, with white diamonds, yellow, orange, cognac and cabochon ruby eyes by Jacob & Co.
Top right: Mitza ring by Dior.
Above: Kenneth Jay Lane. Panther brooch by Kenneth Jay Lane.

The Duchess of Windsor (1896–1986)

Wallis Simpson amassed a vast collection of Cartier's great cat jewels, which she wore like precious pets on leashes of brilliant-cut diamonds, pinning them to a Mainbocher designed dress or clipping them to the lapel of a tweed jacket. Cartier's first panther, in yellow gold and black enamel crouching on a 116.74-carat emerald cabochon stone, was bought for her by the Duke. This first acquisition was quickly followed by opulent naturalistic cats with dazzling yellow diamond eyes sitting on a 152.35-carat sapphire, articulated onyx and diamond-stalking panther bracelets, slumbering cats with pear-shaped emerald eyes and yellow diamond tigers with their diamond forepaws and tails extending around her wrist. 'The lorgnette has returned to fashion. The Duchess of Windsor … is especially fond of a pair which springs out from a small tiger handle of gold, striped in black enamel, emerald eyed', commented *Vogue* in 1955.

Above: The Duchess of Windsor enjoying an evening at the Lido on 11 December 1959. She is wearing her Tiger bracelet made by Cartier in 1956.
Below left: Bracelet by David Webb.
Below right: Bracelet by David Webb.
Bottom: Panther clip brooch, Cartier Paris, 1949.

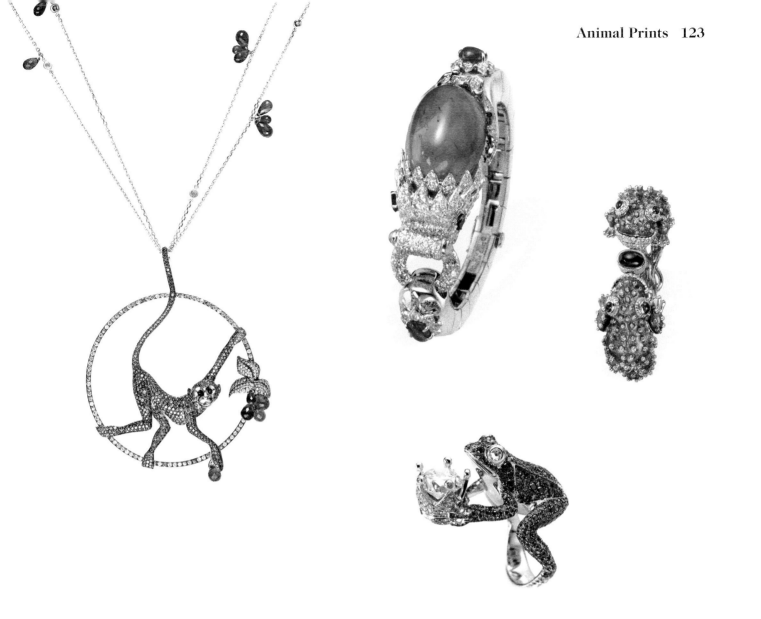

Jeanne Toussaint (1887–1978)

In 1920s' Paris Jeanne Toussaint was renowned for her style and good taste: in turbans draped with long ropes of pearls and her daily uniform of navy blue or Chinese silk pyjamas for the evening she stepped out with friends such as the fashionable portrait painters Giovanni Boldini and Paul Helleu. It was said she was the first woman to wear a tiger coat made by Revillon with pelts from Kenya. When she became his Director of Fine Jewellery in 1933 Louis Cartier called her 'the Panther' because of her ruthless creativity. Using a black-and-gold striped vanity case as inspiration she created the *Panthère* collection of jewels for Cartier, exhibited in 1949. 'Mademoiselle Toussaint's sensational new items', described a contemporary journalist, 'is like an atomic bomb in the central display case … within two hours all of Paris had heard about the panther'. Over the years Cartier and Toussaint's cats have captivated successive audiences with their three-dimensional movement and suppleness, glistening with tens of thousands of tiny stones clinging to the sculpted muscles of the animals. Like chameleons they adapt for new generations, transforming themselves from sensuous tame creatures to sleek contemporary yellow gold wild cats with menacing open mouths.

Top left: Monkey pendant, Animal World collection by Chopard.
Top right: Bracelets by David Webb.
Centre: Frog with Crown ring, Animal World Collection by Chopard
Above: Jeanne Toussaint, Artistic Director of Jewellery at Cartier.

Organic Style

> *'Makers are looking at nature, using its wonders whether it's from sea, earth or the animal kingdom for self-adornment. This approach binds the wearer of the jewel to that source.'*

Julia Muggenburg

The earliest 'jewellery', such as animal bones, teeth or claws, were worn as trophies, in the belief that traits from these animals, such as their strength or speed, would transfer to the wearer. And the same principle is at work in the current trend for organic jewels. Fashion always reflects culture, and so it is no surprise that global environmental issues have provided inspiration for modern designers. Golden-dipped leaves, twigs and freshly dug organic-looking vegetables and ripe fruit jewels connect their wearers, as in prehistory, to the earth. On woodland walks through the Savernake Forest in Wiltshire Philippa Holland collects roebuck antlers, daisy chains, ivy and oak leaves to cast into English folk-themed jewellery. Diamond *Poppy Seed* rings and golden leaf *Breeze* cuffs by Annoushka tangle around fingers and wrists as if they have been blown by the wind. Young jeweller Victoria Tryon's collection resembles a nostalgic walk through an English garden brimming with pussy willow, dandelions, geraniums and acorns; while Italian jeweller Tito Pedrini, inspired by pomegranates ripened in the Mediterranean sun, makes mammoth shiny skinned kernels of fruit in ivory and black onyx with luscious slithers of vivid purple pink and orange sapphire seeds inside. The Chinese landscape is depicted in the black-and-white diamond ear panels by Taipei jeweller Cindy Chao, who creates *Four Seasons* art jewels which reflect the forces of nature with elegant bare branches in black diamonds among mid-winter diamond snowflakes, and spring-like seed pearls budding around a finely set pink pearl. In tune with the country girl theme Chanel recently created a bucolic organic fantasy in the shape of a gigantic hay barn in the Grand Palais in Paris where models wore *broderie anglaise* headscarves and frayed tweed jackets. Marni's accessories for their retro-coloured long shorts and waxed linen jackets are assemblages of real laurel leaves golden-dipped as leaf necklaces, bone and horn discs, and burnt-wood-dusted rings with crushed stone.

Top left: Pomegranate earrings by Tito Pedrini.
Top right: Ring by Lydia Courteille.
Above: From the Four Seasons collection by Cindy Chao.

Bees

Top left to right: Bee earring, ring and pendant by Chaumet.
Centre left: Ring by Dior.
Centre: Vintage bee at SJ Phillips.
Centre right: Mythology bumblebee amulet by Annoushka.

The current worldwide honeybee crisis has encouraged urban dwellers to keep beehives — and has seen a swarm of golden bees emerging from designers' studios. Chosen by Napoleon I as his emblem and worn as a vast jewelled clasp in the shape of a bee which secured his travel cape, the bee is traditionally a symbol of power. Jewellers to Napoleon and his Empress Josephine, Chaumet are using his emblem in a contemporary collection to support campaign group Terre d'Abeilles, who are working to protect bees and nurture their hives. The busy-looking insects in citrine, amethyst and pink opal flap their delicate wings on rings, gather pollen from golden hearts and buzz around earlobes. Their unique ruby and pink spinel queen bee rests on a ring, fanning her outstretched pink gold diamond-set wings. Alex Monroe's gold bumblebee was modelled on a bee caught by his daughters in Suffolk; and for Carolina Bucci the bee symbolises 'virtue', so she attaches a tiny bumblebee charm to her gold and silk woven bracelets and necklaces.

Pippa Small (1968–)

Anthropologist Pippa Small's interest in jewels began as a young 'recycler' as she threaded her treasure trove of minerals, shells, beads, sea-washed glass buttons and gems onto bracelets. Her arms jangle with golden breadfruits and star fruits, jostling alongside aquamarine cardamom and pumpkin seeds, acorns and peppercorns, reflecting her vision of an Indian garden. Her jewels have an 'organic' style, using uncut gems and flat-cut semi-precious stones such as labradorites, opals and slices of tourmaline wrapped in rich yellow Indian gold. Her anthropological background fuels the craft initiatives she undertakes with indigenous communities such as the San Bushman in the Kalahari and the Kuna Indians in Panama. Her work helps them research their traditional designs and generates self-sufficiency. To combat extreme poverty in the slums of Nairobi, Small has created recycled brass necklaces for Made at Nicole Farhi: 'We melt down anything we can find to use', she says, 'like keys, pipes and taps'.

Above: Pippa Small.
Below left: Necklace by Pippa Small for Made.
Below right: Turquoise Mountain cuffs by Pippa Small.
Bottom right: Mixed Scatter ring by Pippa Small.
Bottom centre: Rough pyrite Tibetan ring by Pippa Small.

Clockwise from top left: Carottes
brooch in coral, diamonds, sapphires,
tsavorites and yellow gold, and Maïs
brooch in white pearls, diamonds
and yellow gold by Lorenz Bäumer;
Vegetable charms, edamame and
radish at Victoria Tryon.

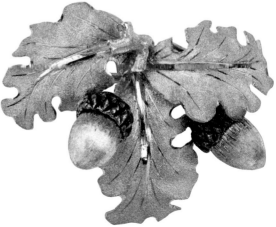

Clockwise from top left: Grapes brooch by Buccellati; Necklace by Marni; Acorns brooch by Buccellati; Leaf brooches by David Morris; Dandelion at Victoria Tryon.

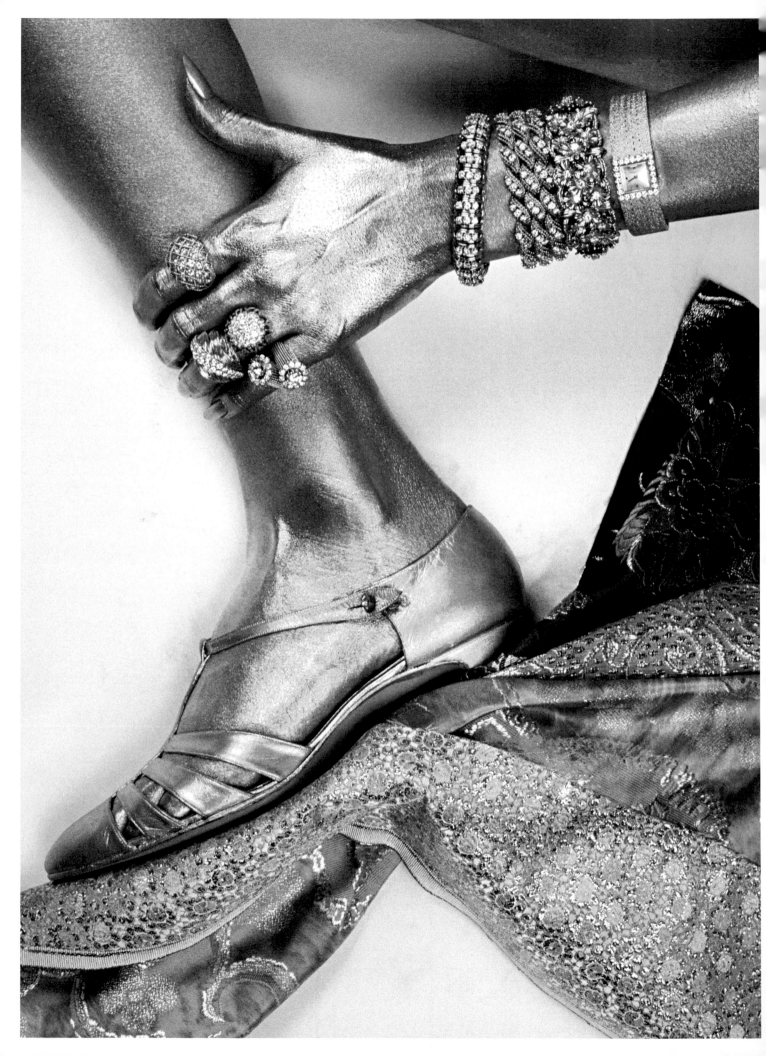

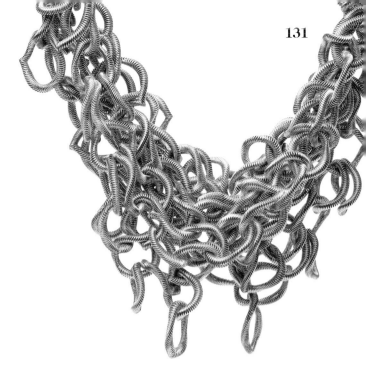

Jewels into Fabrics

'Metallics are innately bold. But this season's dazzling golds are textured, beaten and beaded, creating an even stronger first impression of 24-carat glamour.'

Calgary Avansino

The boundaries between fabric and jewellery become blurred when lace, crochet and knitted fabrics are interpreted by jewellers into softly woven metallic chainmail or golden spiders-web pieces. Prada based a recent collection on the primal appeal of lace: 'It's such an accompaniment of women through their childhood and marriage and being a widow', Miuccia Prada told the London *Times*. Lightly woven fabrics follow the contours of the body in a way that tailored or corseted materials cannot. 'It's about the body, the elastic yarn clings to the body', says knitwear designer Mark Fast, 'it can't be draped'. Fast creates knitwear dresses on domestic knitting machines. The threads of his clothes spin around the body like a sexy spiders' web, exposing a shoulder, thigh or midriff. Like Fast, Lucie Heskett-Brem conjures up webs in her studio overlooking Lake Lucerne, but her silky woven gold strands compose chains that span the neckline like golden gossamer capes. She works in 20-carat yellow gold for its rich buttery colour and malleability which links, knots, twists and intertwines the delicate loops of the chain.

Young goldsmiths such as Andrew Lamb find inspiration in the linear patterns of woven textiles. Lamb's delicate pieces in yellow gold and silver wire are layered and overlapped like a textured tapestry of metal. Catherine Martin spent four years in Japan learning the traditional art of braiding silk called *kumihimo*, an essential element of ceremonial costume and court dress, which she uses in her intricate jewels. Twelve metres of gold and platinum wire unwinding from around twelve bobbins are needed to create one pair of her delicate braided earrings. Carolina Bucci looks to the heritage of Florentine weavers to create her gold and coloured silk cuffs which are woven on a loom that dates back to the Renaissance.

Top left: Brooch by Andrew Lamb.
Top right: 18ct yellow gold necklace by Nina Koutibashvili.

Buccellati

Eighteenth-century Italian jewellers Buccellati create ravishingly delicate brushed and engraved gold jewels with the lightness of linen, silk or delicately threaded Burano lacework. Inspired by Renaissance art their necklaces reproduce graceful wide 17th-century antique lace Venetian collars; their brooches are engraved with gold 'frills' and their precious stone 'tulle' rings set in delicate circles of gold or platinum. They invest their modern-style briolette-cut sapphires and diamonds with a lightness which transforms them into precious rococo pieces of fabric, which might be lace-trimming for a camisole, or tiny lattice-work gold as fine as ribbons.

Above: Tulle necklace by Buccellati.
Below left: Ring by Repossi.
Below right: Lastra bracelet by Buccellati.
Bottom right: Diamond and ruby lace bracelet by Ritz Fine Jewellery.

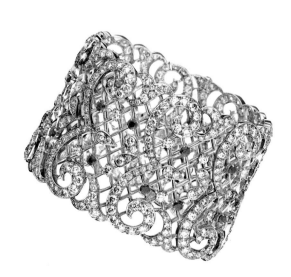

Top left: Bangle with diamonds and white gold by Hemmerle.
Centre right: Bangle with aquamarine, copper and white gold by Hemmerle.
Above left: Bangle with aquamarines, iron and white gold by Hemmerle.
Below: Biker Chain by Ben-Amun for Michael Kors.

Heavy Metal

The House of Hemmerle makes strikingly modern jewellery pieces using brass, copper, textured iron and stainless steel. Juxtaposing a functional 'common' metal with a spectacular, intensely blue aquamarine from Brazil's Santa Maria mine gives their work an intriguing opulence. Stephan Hemmerle experiments with 18th-century oxidation techniques to find the exact shade of copper for an orange diamond; or creates a mottled effect on a copper cuff as the perfect backdrop for a rare topaz. Flawless diamonds and orange melo pearls set into a graphic-shaped iron setting give the stones a powerful aesthetic when worn with metallic burnished gold sequins or Balmain's dirty gold and silver chainmail with heavily hardwared shoulders.

JAR

Described as the greatest living jeweller during his 2002 exhibition at London's Somerset House, Joel Arthur Rosenthal created a magical coloured-carpet technique of setting stones 40 years ago. In 1966 Rosenthal, with his partner Pierre Jeannet, opened a boutique in Paris selling hand-painted tapestry canvasses. This training in embroidery is cited as the influence for his signature pavé work. In this technique, where precious stones are set tightly together, one lilac spray might contain ten-and-a-half thousand stones, the tiny fragments of graduating colours resembling precious needlepoint tapestries. In Rosenthal's artistic hands a rose necklace glistens with a myriad of green tourmalines and garnets with a gently opening diamond dew-dropped bud of pink sapphires and rubies; the wings of an iridescent jewelled butterfly open into vibrant mosaics; and olive-branch brooches in bronzed silver shimmer with green sapphires, tourmalines and peridots as they would in a sunny grove in Toledo. Known for his exacting temperament and attention to detail one particular sprig of lilac took nine years to produce as Rosenthal insisted on sculpting it from the actual flower which only blossoms for a few weeks each year.

Below left: Rose-petal earrings set with pink sapphires, rubies with aluminium gardenia earrings by JAR.
Below right: Topaz pendant earrings with rubies and diamonds by JAR.
Bottom: Black-silver and gold iris brooch with sapphires and diamonds by JAR.
Opposite: Black-silver and gold butterfly brooch with amethysts, blue and pink sapphires and diamonds by JAR.

'*Like his colleagues, Castellani of Rome and Giuliano of Naples, Attilio Codognato was immediately fascinated by the discoveries made at the archaeological digs that were taking place in Etruria at that time*'.

Pierre Hebey

The Classical Look

The stone maidens supporting the Erechtheum on the Acropolis offer a glimpse of what was fashionable in Greece during the 5th century BCE: elongated forms enhanced by intricate gathers and folds. The skilful sculptors created the appearance of transparent drapery on static figures, bringing the sculptures to life through the movement of undulating fabrics. Women's fashion in ancient Rome was the *stola*, a basic garment like a long tunic, with a *palla* scarf or small toga draped across their body, leaving one arm free. This one-shouldered asymmetric neckline, echoing the sensual forms of ancient Greek statues, is also used by modern designers. Lanvin, for example, incorporates Grecian folds into pink, blue and red silks and satins which sweep around the body in pleated swathes, pinned toga-style to one shoulder. Carolina Herrera based her one-shouldered look on the highly idealized romantic female figures of Renaissance paintings such as Botticelli's *Primavera*. Her vivid yellow chiffon frocks float in feminine ruffles around a simple column with petals trailing down to the hem.

Roman accessories included laurel wreaths in the hair, golden hooped earrings, coiled snake bracelets, decorated pins (fibulae) to fasten clothes, carved cameos and gold coins depicting the head of Emperor Marcus Aurelius. Archaeological discoveries during the 19th century sent fashionable women visiting Rome to Castellani, a shop near the Spanish Steps which sold new jewellery inspired by the classical world. Using ancient Etruscan gold, techniques of granulation and filigree and motifs such as urns, shells and ram's heads, Fortunato Pio Castellani created pieces set with ancient Greek and Roman gold coins and Roman micro-mosaic styles based on original pieces discovered in excavations at Orvieto, Knossos and Rhodes.

Top right: Cameo necklace, c. 1800.
Above: Warrior ring by Sevan Bicakci.
Below: Cameo by Lydia Courteille.

Top left: Cameo ring by Lydia Courteille.
Top right: Cameo ring by Dior.
Centre: Elton John cameo ring by Theo Fennell.
Above: Moretto by Codognato.

Cameos

Every year since 1866, when the Casa Codognato opened its doors near St Mark's Square fashionable visitors to Venice have stopped by to view their Roman-inspired jewels, elaborate intaglios and cameos. Prestigious clients include Queen Victoria, painters Manet, Whistler and Renoir, and Coco Chanel dropped in on her way back from the Lido accompanied by Diaghilev. Now modern designers such as Tom Ford and Stefano Pilati make the pilgrimage for classical inspiration. Codognato's famous baroque blackamoor cameos, modelled after a 15th-century gondolier in Venetian artist Vittore Carpaccio's work and named *moretti* after Othello, the Moor of Venice, are carved in ebony with moiré silk turbans, feathered aigrettes and gem-encrusted torsos.

Traditional cameo brooches in the late 19th century were hard stones or shells carved in relief, usually featuring an image of a female classical deity and often based on jewels discovered during excavations at Pompeii and Herculaneum. Stones such as banded agate and even lava from Vesuvius were also used. The carving penetrates several layers of colour, which gives a three-dimensional quality to the work. Cameos have been revived once again in recent times. *Vogue* cover girl Alexa Chung wears a skull cameo with Ralph Lauren dungarees; and Dior's charming garnet, pink tourmaline and agate cameos have a classical beauty as the image on the cameo wears its own pair of dainty diamond-drop earrings. Hemmerle intricately carve black agate cameos into the profile of an Italian noblewoman, hung on an invisibly stitched champagne and smoky quartz necklace, swinging with a tassel of natural pearls.

Coins

During the 1960s Nicola Bulgari, who collected ancient Roman coins, began setting these fragments of antiquity into modern heavy yellow and white gold-link chains and coiled bracelets. 'Coins have immortalized every important person in history', Nicola Bulgari told *Town & Country Magazine*, 'Caesar, Augustus, Nero…'. Bulgari necklaces used coins in bronze, silver and gold from the ancient Mediterranean world as well as modern American coins, scattered with diamonds, which swung on gold chains or faceted citrine beads around the turtlenecks and pantsuits worn at the time. The classical heads in profile are those of the Goddess Roma in armour, Alexander the Great, Medusa, Athena and the Caesars. The texture of the jewellery contrasts the worn matt finish of the ancient coins with the sleek polished highly reflective modern gold surround. Nicola Bulgari was also inspired by the stylised brackets, or parentheses that form patterns on the ancient walkways of the Roman Forum, using them in his bold, geometric *Parentesi* collection.

Below left: Cameo necklace by Bulgari.
Below right: Silver decadrachm of Philip II of Macedonia in pendant by Elizabeth Gage.
Bottom right: Roman coin necklace by Bulgari.

'Brass buttons and braiding let you flirt with forces style, while belted greatcoats and khaki jumpsuits are fit for a new fashion army.'

Vogue, 2007

Regimental Dress

The military look continues to appear on runways with soldierly regularity. Over the years many aspects of service uniforms have been plundered by designers: from gold braid and buttons, to the colours of the British military in India; from dashing revolutionaries such as Che Guevara who still smoulders in khaki and a black beret, to cavalry riding boots, decorative medals and double-breasted red jackets inspired by the Hussars. Yves Saint Laurent, who was the master of feminising masculine trends, dressed Catherine Deneuve in military style for the 1967 film *Belle de Jour*, and controversially showed camouflage colours on the runways during the height of the Vietnam War.

The Burberry trench coat was originally created for officers in the Boer War and World War I who needed protective clothes with latched, waterproof wrists and collars. The modern military Burberry aesthetic includes navy coats, sheepskin-lined aviator jackets, gold buttons and multiple buckles up the sleeves which are lightened by romantic lace mini-dresses and raspberry and gold chiffon dresses. Jewellery too has been influenced by the army: identification tags worn by military personnel — called 'dog tags' — have been made into polished gold and silver fashion accessories. A trend for patriotic jewellery emerges during times of war: for example, Butler & Wilson were inspired to make a myriad of crystal *Union Jack* flag rings, watch dials and *Stars and Stripes* brooches. Their pendulous golden matt drop earrings and gold hoops perfectly balance broad gold-braided epaulette shoulders on new-wave military jackets. Camouflage-coloured gems, such as grass-green demantoid garnets, tourmalines and subtle smoky quartz make a good foil for earthy coloured field drill jackets and button-down battle blouses; and combat-green sequins on Balmain's gold-buttoned tailcoats evoke a 21st-century new model army.

Top left: Stars and Stripes earrings by Bulgari.
Above: Union Jack ring by Butler & Wilson.
Below: Union Jack collection by Butler & Wilson.

Top left: Earrings by
Cassandra Goad.
Centre: Ring by Theo Fennell.
Top right: A gem peridot of 284cts
bordered by pavé-set brilliant-cut
diamonds set in 18ct gold and
platinum by Paloma Picasso
for Tiffany, 1981.
Below: Janet Jackson, 1989.

Janet Jackson (1966–)

Rhythm Nation 1814, Janet Jackson's fourth album, was released in 1989. In
the accompanying video, in soft-focus black-and-white Jackson appeared wearing
a theatrical but menacing button-bedecked black uniform, with broad shoulders,
glistening military decorations and badges, and topped off with a Mao-style black
cap. 'This is a story about control', she announced, 'my control'. The album's multi-
racial message about a better way of life was inspired by youth projects in New York
City founded to create a strong community spirit. Jackson's revolutionary army-style
look, without glitz and glitter, became as powerful as her protest songs, and has inspired
subsequent performers such as Cheryl Cole to adopt a military style.

War Chest

Military history is surprisingly full of stories about jewels; many armies have ridden to war in uniforms paid for with jewellery. The 55.23-carat pear-shaped yellow Sancy diamond, now in the Louvre, was sold in France by Queen Henrietta Maria to fund her husband Charles I's royalist army during the English Civil War. Bequeathed to the French crown by Cardinal Mazarin, it was sold again to support the army during the French Revolution. Scarlett O'Hara in *Gone with the Wind* tosses away her gold wedding ring to be used for the Southern cause. The Prussian royal family appealed to their citizens to donate gold rings to achieve liberation from Napoleon in the early 19th century. The Prussian iron foundries, who produced delicate jewellery like black lace, inscribed 160,000 iron rings with the words 'Gold gab ich für Eisen' to be proudly worn by those who donated to the cause. Iron came to symbolize patriotism and the fight against the enemy, as epitomized by Prussia's highest military honour, the Iron Cross. The requisitioning of metals during war did not diminish the creativity of jewellers Fabergé who created their last imperial egg in steel adorned with gun shells in 1916. Similarly Cartier made 'austerity' tiaras in gunmetal with diamonds and Verdura wrought necklaces from shrapnel.

Above: Dog-tag necklace by Pippa Small.
Below left: Vintage cross at SJ Phillips.
Below right: Prussian iron necklace, c. 1820.

'It's more about a feeling of how women want to feel in their clothes now…wrapped, draped, supported in cocooning shapes. Investment pieces that stand the test of time.'

Amanda Wakeley

Sartorial Security

The primary function of clothes is to provide protection, warmth and security to the body especially during turbulent times, when clothes are the first line of defence in a dark world. Wrapping up in a luxurious smart-looking cashmere coat or cape provides comfort on a physical level, with the cosy feeling of natural fibres next to the skin. And sartorially a classic look is a fail-safe. In times of economic recession smart girls indulge in 'investment dressing', spending wisely on wardrobe staples that will wear well and keep chic through tight times. In the middle of the 2009 global financial crisis *Vogue* announced that 'money-per-wear, a camel coat is the best investment you can make this season'. In such times glitz and glamour are not appropriate, and designers in tune with the mood bring back hard-working understated classic pieces such as pinstripe suits, grey flannel trousers, and tweed jackets. The Jil Sander formula is deliberately classic: it pairs simple turtle-necked dresses with perfectly tailored coats worn with flat shoes. All this scores high for both comfort and chic.

Jewellery which fulfils the desire for security has a resonance beyond status and suggests a deeper significance, such as the Cartier *Love* bangle, dotted with screw motifs, and worn by couples as a love 'handcuff'. Chaumet have revived sentimental 'acrostic' jewels, as worn by the Empress Josephine in the early 1800s. The name of each stone on the bracelet spells out a word to record an emotion or secret message. To accessorise her cocoon coats and smart cropped jackets Amanda Wakeley creates her own jewels. 'My clothes are all about empowering women to make them feel great, and I wanted to do the same with my jewellery', she says. Working in silver to make pieces more affordable for working girls, she sets amethysts, smoky quartz and citrine into simple lozenge and pyramid shapes, stackable diamond and sapphire bands, bi-colour hooped earrings and lariat diamond-drop pendants to create a capsule jewellery wardrobe.

Top: Gold Love bracelet, Cartier New York, 1970.
Above: Horse-bit bracelet in yellow gold by Gucci.

Faith Jewels

During the financial boom of the 1980s Greek jeweller Deppy Chandris made plastic and diamond dollar-sign brooches. Now it is her delicately wrought diamond birds of peace that are sought after. Today's more reflective mood has inspired jewellery made not simply for adornment but to connect the wearer to a deeper path during challenging times, using symbols such as Christian Crosses and the Egyptian ankh. Gucci showed 18th-century-inspired gowns with large black crosses; and Madonna has turned Dolce & Gabbana crosses, rosary beads and crucifixes into fashion accessories worn with corsets and leopard-print dresses. At New York jewellers Satya, Buddhist prayer-beads and Hindu mala make fashionable necklaces sacred. Angel wings on leather cords by Diane Kordas, and Garrard's diamond set pieces are worn as multi-faith symbols of goodness and peace.

Above: Cross by Theo Fennell.
Below left: Devil and Angel Key pendants by Theo Fennell.
Below right: Classic Wings diamond ring by Garrard.
Bottom left: Evil Eye 'Art pendant by Theo Fennell.
Bottom right: Mapplethorpe Crosses by Chrome Hearts.

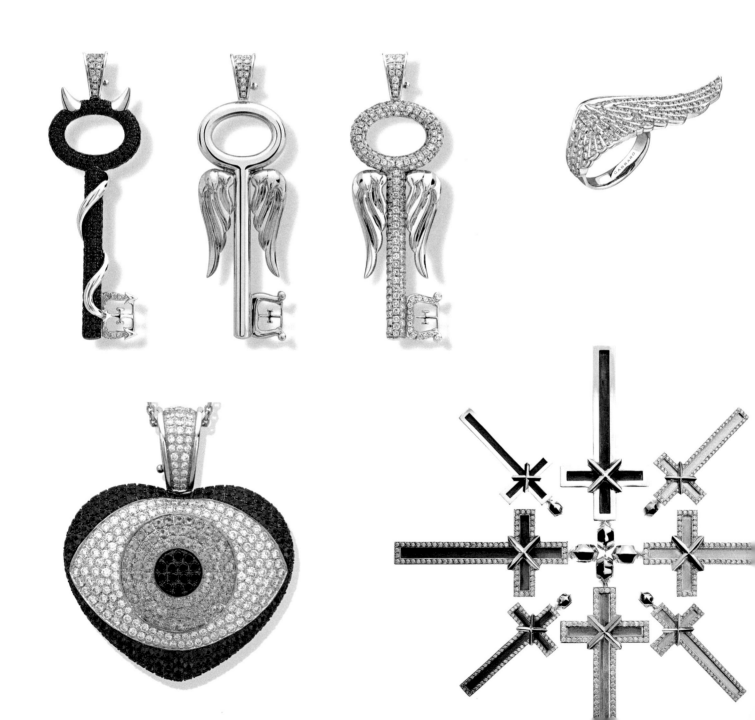

Charms

A charm bracelet is a golden treasury of personal memories, marking important and sentimental moments over a lifetime. It can also carry talismanic pieces to ward off evil. 'In my travels around the world studying the human species I noticed that almost everywhere I went people had some kind of lucky charm', writes Desmond Morris in *Bodyguards*. Elizabeth Taylor's charm bracelet clinks with dozens of hands of Fatima, hearts inscribed with messages, evil eyes, lockets, engraved medallions for each of her children, St Christophers and peace signs. *Touche Bois* are wooden lucky charms by Theo Fennell, hand carved from wood that means something to the wearer, that people literally hold onto in sticky situations — maybe the wooden door from their first home or the favourite oak tree they sat under as a child. Combining love and luck young jeweller Annina Vogel rifles through vintage stores for whimsical Victorian charms which she hangs on modern chain-linked necklaces twinkling with diamond-set four-leaf clovers, shamrocks and hearts. 'People like to find something with meaning to them', she says.

Top left: Yellow gold Touche Bois pendants with wood from the decks of HMS Victory by Theo Fennell.
Centre left: Diamond Petals Key set in platinum by Tiffany.
Centre right: Fiancée du Vampire by Dior.
Top right: Diamond Love and Luck necklace by Annina Vogel.
Above: Charm bracelet by Louis Vuitton.

'From under his artfully chaotic hair, two sapphire and diamonds twinkle in his ears; a trip of bracelets circle his wrist; and under the tautly fitted shirt is a belt with a buckle that looks like a Hell's Angel has mated with a goth night-clubber.'

Suzy Menkes on Stephen Webster

The Rock Star

Rock stars have influenced modern men's fashion since the 1960s when The Rolling Stones abandoned conservative suits for hard-edged skinny jeans and leather jackets. But the rock-star look can be traced back much further to Romantic poet Lord Byron — 'mad, bad and dangerous to know' according to his mistress Lady Caroline Lamb. Byron's soft pointed ruffled shirts with lace collars were worn almost as a form of ornamental jewellery. The style was adopted during the 1980s by New Romantic bands such as Adam and the Ants who added streaky eyeliner, spiked hair and gold-embroidered military-style jackets to create the look of a band of swashbuckling buccaneers. To develop her 1980s *Pirate* collection, Vivienne Westwood (who designed for Adam and the Ants) fused romantic ideas of billowing shirts with historically accurate patterns of 18th-century men's clothing which she researched at London's Victoria & Albert Museum.

Top left: Karl Lagerfeld's hands wearing rings by Chrome Hearts Homme, Dior Homme and Chanel. **Above:** Bracelets by Chrome Hearts. **Below:** Johnny Depp, 2007. **Opposite:** Self-portrait by Karl Lagerfeld, February 2010.

The rock-star-meets-pirate look relies on retro shades, leather, a touch of Lurex and elaborately worked silver chains, rings and bangles with dark themes such as skulls, swords, daggers and gothic crosses. The archetypal bad-boy rock star is Rolling Stone Keith Richards. For his appearance in the film *Pirates of the Caribbean* alongside Johnny Depp (who based his performance as Captain Jack Sparrow on Richards) Keith wore tattered jeans, a billowing piratical shirt and a bandana — virtually the same costume he wears as lead guitarist of The Rolling Stones. He also wears a pair of small silver handcuffs on his wrist, 'as a reminder', he says, 'to never get arrested again'. Couture rocker, Karl Lagerfeld, who dresses in leather skinny jeans with a black tie around a stiff high white starched collar, has several drawers full of silver rings, and wears up to 23 at a time. An old signet from his mother is mixed up with ornate highly patterned heavy medieval-style rings by Chrome Hearts, and his tie is held in place by a diamond Van Cleef & Arpels brooch. Influenced by his Spanish heritage John Galliano, who frequently explores historic themes in his designs, recently created an 18th-century-meets-rock-star collection with models dressed in blouson shirts, Regency powdered wigs and black velvet overcoats with gold embroidery topped off by tricorne hats.

Skulls

In Elizabethan England the death's head emblem was worn by rakes and sexual adventurers crafted onto wide silver bands which they rotated on their fingers, to be hidden when necessary, or displayed in the company of a potential conquest. Keith Richards had his silver skull ring sculpted by Master Goldsmiths Courts & Hackett from a miniature sculpture of a real human skeleton. He wears it, he says, as a reminder 'that beauty is only skin deep'. The transience of life is depicted in the gold and ivory skull rings, memento mori and skeleton pendants created by fourth-generation Venetian jeweller Codognato. Their darkly brooding style draws on Dutch 17th-century still-life *vanitas* paintings which used symbols such as skulls, hour-glasses and snuffed candles to comment on the futility of human existence. Theo Fennell infuses his skull rings with humour by placing a pair of aviator sunglasses or a tiny diamond tiara on their heads. The skulls by Victoire de Castellane at Dior, sculpted in hardstone lavender and green jade, are elaborately dressed in diamond-encrusted Byron-style ruffled collars with ornate regal crowns and plumed headdresses.

Above: Skull pendant by Codognato.
Below: Carved mammoth-bone skull ring by Theo Fennell.
Right: Skull brooch by Dior.
Far right: Keith Richards' silver skull ring by Courts & Hackett.

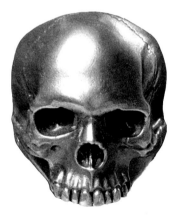

Loree Rodkin

With a style described as 'medieval meets modern' Los Angeles designer Loree Rodkin creates jewelled daggers, claws and skulls in brooding brown and rough-cut diamonds, emphasising their dark and subversive nature. She began designing and making jewels when, as a talent manager, she waited for long hours to bail her client, Robert Downey Jr., out of trouble. Her bondage-style diamond knuckleduster rings are articulated to span the length of the finger, while sinister diamond skull rings stare out from two large black diamond eyes with a wicked piratical smile, as a smaller black diamond glints from its teeth.

Top left: Yellow gold gothic cross by Loree Rodkin.
Centre right: Solid pavé bondage ring by Loree Rodkin.
Above left: Sabre pendant by Loree Rodkin.
Above right: Diamond skull ring by Loree Rodkin.

Unbridled Leather

'I see leather as unisex, fairly interchangeable.'

Pascale Mussard, Hermès

Leather has always been used in clothing: ancient cave paintings show women wearing leather animal hides, and the Romans popularized its use throughout their empire in both footwear and clothes. Prized for their warmth and thick protective quality, leather jackets took on a military meaning during the 20th century. The 'bomber' jacket was worn by real-life action heroes such as Douglas Bader as well as those acting heroic on celluloid such as Tom Cruise in *Top Gun*. After World War II the leather jacket attained iconic status among British and American youth when worn with denims by Marlon Brando in *The Wild One* and became associated with the 'live fast, die young' ethos of Elvis Presley and James Dean. And the traditional Belstaff Hero racer-style jacket is still associated with the macho Hell's Angels biking brigade.

But modern designers are today giving leather a ladylike spin, working it into less severe, more supple feminine forms. Rodarte create cobweb-like dresses in leather and lace, and Christopher Kane embellishes black leather mini-dresses with spring flowers in diagonal fine black lace panels, turning hardcore leather into something pretty and elegant. Peter Pilotto and Christopher de Vos set leather in a modern context, mixing up tweed, orange hides and metallic silver fabric in cardigans and softly draping dresses. A tangle of strong-looking but refined Hermès *Chaîne d'ancre*, wrapped several times around the wrist, emphasises street-smart chic. Hoorsenbuhs, whose Los Angeles atelier is located in a structure commissioned by the US army during World War II, make tri-link black diamond chain necklaces, and also craft super-soft small versions of leather belts with gold diamond buckles to wind three times around the arm. Juxtaposing a whisper of delicate vintage-inspired precious diamond drop earrings by De Beers or Stephen Webster with a tough urban style gives leather an unexpected twist.

Top left: Strap cuffs by Hoorsenbuhs.
Top right: Chesterfield Hunter's Bangle by Tomasz Donocik.
Centre: Astral 2 bangle by Hermès.
Above: Lily Cole wearing Hermès, 2010.

Thierry Hermès (1801–78)

Thierry Hermès opened a harness and bridle workshop in Paris in 1837 where he produced *Haut à Courroies* bags so that riders could carry their saddles with them. These early sporty saddle-bags were gradually transformed into the elegant Kelly handbag, named for Grace Kelly who carried one, and Birkin bags (named for Jane Birkin) which fashionistas have an annual fight to get their hands on. 'We can borrow numerous accessories from men, then transform, adapt and feminise them', says designer Pierre Hardy. 'I like the idea of this "transgressive" aspect.' The bags are produced in the chic glass Hermès workshops outside Paris where vibrant-coloured dyed skins are meticulously cut. Drawing on their equestrian heritage, Hermès saddle-stitch by hand, two needles working together through precisely judged perforations. Ostrich, Chamonix calf-leather, bridle leather, natural lizard and alligator — it takes two of these to make a Kelly bag — are turned into elegant purses and coordinating pieces of jewellery. The *Kelly Double Tour* and *Kelly 'Dog'* leather bracelets wrap around the wrist with a metal-tipped clasp closed with a tiny diamond padlock; and the *Clochette* necklace, like the Birkin bag, has a key enclosed in a lanyard which loops through the leather.

Emma Peel

Actress Diana Rigg will forever be remembered for her role as fictional spy, Emma Peel, in the television programme *The Avengers* during the 1960s, reprised by Uma Thurman in *The Avengers* film of 1998. Emma Peel (the name was said to be a pun on 'M-Appeal') was a formidable fencer and master of martial arts, which suited the tough styling of her tight black leather pantsuits. The soft leather cut also gave her flexibility of movement in her athletic action scenes. A feminist heroine, Peel carried an Italian Beretta pistol and drove a Lotus Elan sports car in pale powder blue, while wearing an Edwardian-style black corset with long, kinky leather boots. Peel's skin-tight patent-leather suits glinted with chunky silver buckles and zips. Out of character in her civilian clothes, however, Rigg preferred 'uncut coloured diamonds and great globs of gold'. With the advent of colour television Peel began to dress in bright bold Mod patterns, but she will remain engrained in the psyche of a generation as a high-kicking leather-clad cat woman.

Above: Uma Thurman as the new Emma Peel.
Below left to right: Coeur bracelet by Louis Vuitton; Astral cuff by Hermès; cuff by Sevan Bicakci; leather and diamond cuff by Tomasz Donocik.

Fringes and Fastenings

'We transform the ornaments and accessories of High Fashion into something eternal; glimmering gold lace, pom-poms in precious stones, ribbons blazing with rubies, magical diamond zippers....'

Stanislas de Quercize, Van Cleef & Arpels

Fashion designers have always delighted in twisting buttons, belts, fringes and zips — the utilitarian fastenings of clothes — into an elaborate feature rather than just a simple necessity. Jewellery designers also mimic fabric fastenings, manipulating metal into gem-encrusted bows, diamond tassels and buckles which turn purely functional items into precious objects with a high glamour quotient. Women's daytime jewellery in the 18th century included precious shoe buckles, worn high on the ankle, which were set with diamonds and sapphires, ribbons and silver rococo scrollwork. They became so elaborate that in 1777 Sheridan's Lord Foppington in *A Trip to Scarborough* commented that, although buckles were meant to keep a shoe on, 'the case is now quite reversed and the shoe is no earthly use, but to keep on the buckle'.

New century diamond buckles feature in heavy-linked *Boucle Sellier* bracelets by Hermès and highly stylised sharp black enamel and pink lacquer cuffs by Shaun Leane. Sotheby's Diamonds creates rubber necklaces which fasten with large pear-shaped diamond buttons; and boutonnière rings and bracelets by Van Cleef & Arpels are threaded through their centres with extravagant ruby strands. The soft fringes on recent cocktail dresses by Alberta Ferretti and Roberto Cavalli swing with a 'flapper' appeal and echo the shimmering embellished evening dresses, long chains and tassels on the onyx, coral and seed-pearls sautoirs of the 1920s. Coco Chanel created a diadem in 1932 which was literally a diamond-cut fringe hung low touching the brow, and a *Fountain* necklace, which has been recreated in a chic contemporary style, hanging low to the waist like a platinum bell cord, swinging with its brilliant fringed tassel.

Top left: Vintage bow brooch at SJ Phillips.
Top right: Necklace by David Morris.
Above: Franges necklace in white gold with diamonds by Chanel Fine Jewellery.

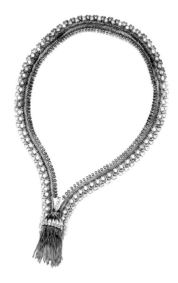

Zips

By making them in a variety of colours Elsa Schiaparelli was one of the first couturiers to draw attention to the humble zip fastener. This fashion inspired the Duchess of Windsor in 1938 to ask Van Cleef & Arpels to make a platinum zip necklace with baguette-cut diamonds. Called *Zip* the necklace is made today in glittering rows of different cuts of diamonds which echo the ornamental ironwork of the Eiffel Tower. At Van Cleef & Arpels polished lace-effect zippers like gold fabric are hung with braided cords, white metal cuffs zip up arms like a slide fastener, and the fancy diamond teeth of some are set onto mink chokers. In the same manner as Schiaparelli modern fashion designers now expose industrial-looking metallic zips for decorative effect. Gucci uses 'scuba' plastic zips with chunky plastic teeth on dresses alongside black-effect diamond zip-shaped necklaces shimmering with chains. Industrial-style zips have become a motif for the House of Lanvin, and add an edge which toughens up their frothy chiffon light-as-a-feather creations trailing with flounces, fringes and frills.

Above and below centre: Zip necklaces by Van Cleef & Arpels. **Bottom left:** Black galuchat zip necklace by Van Cleef & Arpels. **Bottom right:** Zip bracelet by Wartski.

Bows

Nobody had more elaborate diamond-set buckles, tassels and bows than Marie Antoinette who wore magnificent ethereal webs of diamonds in tasselled ribbons across her breast. Empress Eugénie fashioned her jewels after Marie Antoinette's style with even more flamboyant and extravagant ivy-patterned bow-knots suspended over streaming diamond pampilles cords. In 1887, when catalogues were distributed for the sale of the French crown jewels, the royal bow-knots were mimicked by jewellers around the world, and are still knotted with a flourish by contemporary fine jewellers. Georgina Chapman for Marchesa designs ultra-romantic long dresses which fall like molten gold lace, with large bows balanced on the shoulders for a modern Marie Antoinette's red-carpet moment. She re-creates the look using looped diamond bow-knot earrings, falling with cascades of diamonds. Dior create charming bow-shaped *Débutante* diamond necklaces, as well as 'undone' versions, where the diamond ribbons fall loose for a dishevelled look at the end of the ball. H. Stern's bows have shimmery brown diamond laces hanging like undone corsetry which resemble the loose-latticed dress bodices at Céline.

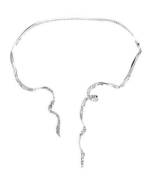

Top left: Yellow gold pendant by Van Cleef & Arpels.
Top right: Pink sapphire and diamond bow ring by Ritz Fine Jewellery.
Centre left: Ribbon brooches by Ritz Fine Jewellery.
Centre right: Necklace by Van Cleef & Arpels.
Above: Diamond necklace by Dior.

'Fashion is architecture: it is a matter of proportions.'

Coco Chanel

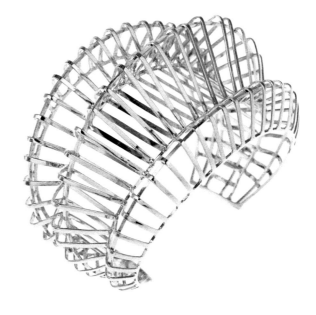

Structured Dressing

Architecture and fashion both reflect the urban zeitgeist in their shape, volume and dramatic silhouettes. As both arts aim to reconcile expressive form with function they also share a language of texture, shape and structure. Equally there are techniques which flow between both media, such as the architect's engineering and construction methods, the couturier's weaving, draping and folding and the goldsmith's texturing and metalwork. While many buildings today have adopted a fashion-like fluidity, visible in the swooping curves and folds of Frank Gehry's Guggenheim Museum in Bilbao, the fabric work employed by Viktor & Rolf or Alexander McQueen's metal fibre cocoon shapes create almost architecturally stiff structures. Japanese designer Yohji Yamamoto uses whalebone to construct a bustier dress as if it is a solid structure, flaring it outwards with suspension straps between the hips and shoulders to distribute weight. Both jewellers and architects explore new metals such as titanium, used to clad Gehry's buildings, the thin copper pleats on Herzog & de Meuron's Central Signal Box in Basel, or the zinc-covered Jewish Museum in Berlin by Daniel Libeskind. Alisa Moussaieff's oversized gem-encrusted brooches are also made in light-weight titanium, the jewels balancing on thin metal. The 'barbed-wire' effect of huge coloured titanium hooped earrings by Suzanne Syz echoes Gehry's use of mundane metals such as chain-link fencing and chicken wire. Architecture has been described as one part maths and one part art and Solange Azagury-Partridge based her *Platonic* collection on mathematical forms using geometry to generate the diamond shapes. Like a miniature Meccano set, the criss-cross effect of the diamond-structured paving on an Hermès cuff is inspired by the metal architecture of the Eiffel Tower.

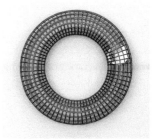

Top left: Grace ring by Jacqueline Rabun.
Top right: 18ct yellow gold Trapezium bracelet by Carol Kauffman.
Above: Earrings by Suzanne Syz. Grace round bangle by Jacqueline Rabun.

Hussein Chalayan (1970–)

Hussein Chalayan's interest in fashion was motivated by his fascination for the human body. 'Buildings are like bodies to me', he says, 'they have a system, a centre, drainage'. Inspired by the science, technology and architecture of Le Corbusier, Herzog & de Meuron and Oscar Niemeyer Chalayan combines meticulous cutting with new techniques. Drawn to innovative materials he has used fabric from aircraft construction for a dress which changes shape by remote control. He takes utilitarian fabrics such as cardboard, neoprene and rubber and emblazons them with prints of tough urban scenes depicting concrete, fencing, scaffolding and iron girders set into silk panels and metallic tweeds. His most famous installation showed three models transforming their garments into wood-veneer pieces of furniture.

Above: Hussein Chalayan prêt-à-porter, autumn/winter 2009.
Below left: Ring by Baccarat.
Below right: Segment cuff in ebony and silver by Gerda Lynngarrd.
Bottom: Bold collection by Cora Sheibani.

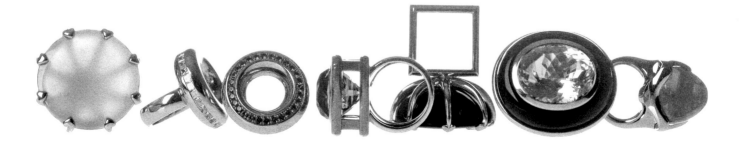

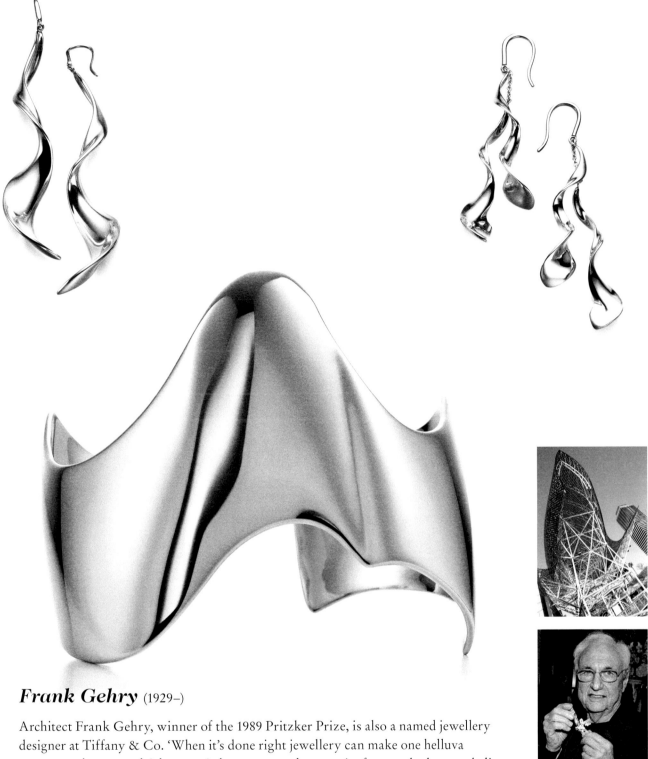

Frank Gehry (1929–)

Architect Frank Gehry, winner of the 1989 Pritzker Prize, is also a named jewellery designer at Tiffany & Co. 'When it's done right jewellery can make one helluva statement about people', he says, 'who you are, where you're from and what you believe in'. The theme of feminine identity emerges in Gehry's buildings, for example the steel-clad form on the top of Bard College's Performing Arts Center, which is redolent of a corset Madonna might have worn on stage during the 1980s. These free-form revolutionary architectural shapes on a grand scale form the central reference point for his jewellery: softly curving *Torque* bangles in sculptural wood, jadeite, onyx, and quartz; *Equus* squiggle-shapes and large silver fish on cords inspired by Brancusi sculptures. Gehry uses fashion as an inspiration, cutting out pictures of skirts from *Vogue*: 'We're doing this hotel where the condos overlap to form a tiered, skirt-like effect. I saw this picture and it inspired me'.

Top left and right: Orchid earrings in sterling silver by Frank Gehry for Tiffany & Co.
Centre: Flux cuff in 18ct yellow gold by Frank Gehry for Tiffany & Co.
Above: The Fish with the Mapfre Tower in the distance by Frank Gehry. Frank Gehry with his jewellery collection for Tiffany & Co.

Fantasy Island

*'Psychedelic prints are wild, hot and madly stylised;
a grab-bag of sinuous Art Nouveau blooms, Op art
graphics and Arabian exotica.'*

James Sherwood

Influenced by psychedelic art on concert posters, murals and album covers (such as Santana's *Abraxas*), which in turn was inspired by the effects of mind-expanding drugs, the 1960s heralded a fashion for fantasy colours in exploding bursts of neon-coloured pattern. Italian aristocrat and designer Emilio Pucci introduced the psychedelic look into mainstream fashion with his signature prints which used 150 bright colours in distinctive curved patterns. A glamorous post-war figure who captured the imagination of the modern woman, Pucci set up his couture house at his family's Florentine palazzo and brought a jet-set cachet to his clothes.

The 21st-century Pucci girl on today's runways, in Pucci's signature coloured-print swimwear, glamorous cover-ups and billowing djellabas, still looks as if she lounges on fantasy islands off the Italian Riviera. Computer art and the digital revolution — described by Timothy Leary as the 'new LSD' — has sparked a psychedelic renaissance with tinsel-trimmed tie-dyed abstract animal-print ruffled minis at Proenza Schouler, and strapless mini-dresses in eye-popping green, blue and yellow prints described by Donatella Versace as 'Alice in Wonderland going into Versace's world'. Punchy design duo Legge & Braine make psychedelic super-sized rings from Venetian Murano glass in a collection called *Granny Drops Acid*. Bright technicolour kaleidoscope patterns swirl around their cup-cake-sized flamboyant rings. The jewels in the showroom of surfing enthusiast and Parisian jeweller Lorenz Bäumer, inspired by catching waves in Fiji, Costa Rica and the island of Kauai, take the form of graceful diamond birds, exuberant bangles of fruity pink opal and mandarin garnets bursting with sumptuous ruby seeds and pavé-set berries. A paisley-patterned ring is anchored by an aquamarine surrounded by psychedelic circles of pink sapphires, swirls of green garnets and sputnik-like splashes of vivid orange and red, evoking the fauna and flora of a lush fantasy island rock garden.

Top left: Pink Pagoda ring by Wendy Yeu.
Top right: Idylle à Moyobamba bracelet/brooch by Dior.
Centre: Brooch by Van Cleef & Arpels.
Above: Granny Drops Acid ring by Legge & Braine.

Above: Victoire de Castellane.
Below left and centre: Belladone Island necklace and brooch by Victoire de Castellane for Dior.
Below right and bottom: Milla Carnivora Ancolia rings by Victoire de Castellane for Dior.

Victoire de Castellane

At Dior Victoire de Castellane creates fanciful blossoms and captivating creatures throbbing with vibrant three-dimensional colour: 'I love coloured stones', she says. 'They are like sweets, I feel I can taste them.' Her magnificent *Reina Magnifica Sangria* necklace is smothered in Paraiba tourmalines, rubies and demantoid garnets which grow from a twisted lacquer stem of deadly diamond berries. The pieces are beautiful but they may also be poisonous — hence she names them *Belladone Island*. Some flowers in her glistening garden are inspired by carnivorous plants: 'The flowers are really feminine, yet really strange, not classical', she says. Their poisonous nature is given a high-octane glamorous makeover with electric-coloured rubies, emeralds, spinels, garnets, opals and tourmalines. Many contain a hidden treasure like the petals of a blue-grey flower encrusted with diamond dust which open to reveal a big spinel stone, or a butterfly resting on a ring which pops out its dazzling coloured-stone wings.

Island Pearls

In the warm waters around the islands of the Caribbean the Queen Conch produces rare salmon-pink pearls. It is one of the rarest pearls in the world: only one in ten thousand of these large sea snails produces a pearl. Coated in a silky veneer these pearls' colour chart ranges from blush pink to luminous candy shades. David Morris arranges the pearls in delicate beds of soft rose-cut diamonds with rare natural white pearls in modern Deco parures, and sets off the bright orange-coloured melo pearl in ring shanks of contrasting yellow diamonds. The fiery-looking ping-pong-ball-shaped melo pearl, which is thought to be a symbol of wisdom in ancient Chinese iconography, is produced by a marine snail which lives in the South China Seas.

Above and below left: South Sea pearl earrings and necklace by David Morris.
Below right: Brooch by Cartier
Bottom centre: Melo pearl and yellow diamond ring by David Morris.

'It's easily overlooked that what is now called vintage was once brand new.'

Tony Visconti

Vintage

Vintage clothes possess an aesthetic from another time, which could be as recent as a Diane von Furstenberg wrap dress from the 1980s, or as far back as a rare 1890s' gown by Charles Worth. A vintage look can be a carbon-copy clone of granny's style or a simple retro tweak of individuality within contemporary fashion. John Galliano has used the glamour of 1940s' *film noir* as inspiration, citing smouldering Lauren Bacall as the muse for his silver lamé dresses: 'She was a great Dior client — there are amazing photos of her in the salon with Bogart'. L'Wren Scott has looked back to Madame du Barry, Louis XV's mistress, evoking a pink-tinted, frothy Versailles look, mixed with her precisely tailored sheath dresses. Scott's Victorian vintage is evident in cutaway jackets with high ruffled collars shown with Fred Leighton's beautiful 19th-century old-cut diamond jewels.

Chiming with the new era of re-cycling — and as a protest against high-street fashion homogeneity — charity-shop chic has become fashionable. 'Thrifting', which used to be called 'second-hand', has assumed a superior status and become a new pastime. Annoushka Ducas bases her jewellery collection on her mother's pieces accumulated during her lifetime. 'I like mixing old and new and layering as you would do with clothes', she says of her vintage-looking rose quartz rings and chrysophrase earrings which are designed to look 'inherited'. Jewellers use subtly coloured gunmetal-grey or black gold to achieve 'that slightly vintage look as if your jewellery has a past', explains Ducas. H. Stern's *Victoriana* collection delicately references Queen Victoria's sombre dresses and dark jewels, shimmering with brown diamonds set into their own mix of vintage 'noble' gold to give a worn, antique look.

Top left: Vintage aquamarine and diamond necklace at Sandra Cronan.
Top right: Vintage emerald, pearl and diamond necklace at Sandra Cronan.
Above: Pink topaz pendant by Fabergé.

Above: Alexander McQueen, autumn/winter 2008/09.
Top: Eggs by Fabergé.
Above left: Blue topaz brooch by Fabergé.
Above right: Aquamarine brooch by Fabergé.

Peter Carl Fabergé (1846–1920)

Jeweller and goldsmith to the Russian tsars, Peter Carl Fabergé, made luxurious fantasy objects such as animals and vases of flowers carved in hard stones, boxes, clocks, and cigarette cases as well as jewellery in an elaborate 18th-century French rococo style. Between 1882 and 1917, using 500 skilled craftsmen in Moscow and Saint Petersburg, Fabergé became a huge producer of jewels and unique objects, many cut into previously unseen shapes. Fabergé's engravers, metal workers and enamellers were encouraged to use different colours of gold such as red, green and yellow in startling new designs. They used soft, rose-cut diamonds as enhancement for the dark green beauty of Russia's native jade and set mesmerising deep-coloured Siberian sapphires and amethysts into discreet diamond borders. For Tsar Alexander II Fabergé made a magnificent white and gold egg, like a Russian matryoshka doll, with a gold yolk inside which opened to reveal a hen who was hiding a tiny crown hanging with a ruby. Until the workshops were closed down during the Revolution Fabergé created egg treasures for the Russian royal family as well as tiny egg-jewelled trinkets to be worn around the neck. Alexander McQueen led the recent Romanov revival, showing a crimson lacquered Fabergé-style egg-shaped handbag with a matching satin high-ruffled-collar evening coat, as well as eagle-skull headdresses containing nests of silver and gemstone Fabergé eggs.

Angela Tassoni (1972–)

Influenced by her Italian heritage of classical architecture, Renaissance art and baroque tapestries Arizona-born designer Angela Tassoni began making vintage necklaces to alleviate the boredom of her teenage modelling assignments: 'One way to make my photographs look unique was to wear my own jewellery', she said. She scours antique markets around the world collecting vintage buckles, pendants, butterflies and cameos by collectable names from the early 20th century. Weiss, Eisenberg and Trifari are her favourites: they rose to prominence during the 1930s and 1940s, making glamorous Hollywood-style pieces with fine rhinestones, crystal and black enamel. Tassoni strings these *objets trouvés* onto semi-precious-stone and bead necklaces, like intricate jewelled collars — a vintage centrepiece with a modern aesthetic and spirit.

Above: Angela Tassoni in Los Angeles, 2010.
Below: Necklaces by Angela Tassoni.

Index

Numbers in italics refer
to illustrations

Further Reading

Baudot, François. *Chanel.* Paris: Assouline, 2004.

Bäumer, Lorenz. *Le Dictionnaire égoïste de Lorenz Bäumer.* Paris: Editions de la Martinière, 2007.

Bennett, David and Daniela Mascetti. *Understanding Jewellery.* Woodbridge: Antique Collectors' Club, 1989.

Corgnasi, Martina. *Mario Buccellati: Prince of Goldsmiths.* New York: Rizzoli International, 1999.

Fox, Patty. *Star Style at the Academy Awards: A Century of Glamour.* Santa Monica: Angel City Press, 2000.

Gabardi, Melissa. *Jean Després: Jeweller, Maker and Designer of the Machine Age.* London: Thames & Hudson, 2009.

Harlow, George E. (ed.) *The Nature of Diamonds.* Cambridge: Cambridge University Press, 1998.

Hebey. Pierre. *Codognato.* Paris: Assouline, 2003.

Joyce, Kristin and Shellei Addison. *Pearls: Ornament and Obsession.* London: Thames & Hudson, 1992.

Loring, John. *Tiffany in Fashion.* New York: Harry N. Abrams, Inc., 2003.

Menkes, Suzy. *The Royal Jewels.* London: Harper Collins, 1985.

Morris, Desmond. *Body Guards: Protective Amulets and Charms.* London: Harper/Element, 1999.

Mulvagh, Jane. *Vogue: History of 20th-century Fashion.* Harmondsworth: Penguin, 1998.

Munn, Geoffrey C. *Tiaras: A History of Splendour.* Woodbridge: Antique Collectors' Club, 2001.

Nadelhoffer, Hans. *Cartier.* London: Thames & Hudson, 2007.

Petit, Marc. *Van Cleef & Arpels: Reflets d'éternité.* Paris: Editions Cercle d'Art, 2006.

Phillips, Clare. *Jewels and Jewellery.* London: V&A Publications, 2000.

Proddow, Penny and Marion Fasel. *Diamonds: A Century of Spectacular Jewels.* New York: Harry N. Abrams, 1996.

Proddow Penny, Debra Healy and Marion Fasel. *Hollywood Jewels.* New York: Harry N. Abrams, 1992.

Triossi, Amanda and Daniela Mascetti. *Bulgari.* London: Thames & Hudson, 2007.

Westin, Ann. *Torun: Conversations with Vivianna Torun Bülow-Hübe.* Stockholm: Carlsson, 1993.

Wilcox, Claire (ed.) *The Golden Age of Couture.* Paris and London, 1947–57. London: V&A Publications, 2007.

Acknowledgements and Picture Credits

Author's Acknowledgements
Grateful thanks to the jewellery industry in London, the haute joaillerie and fashion houses in Paris and in other cities around the world for generously supplying images of their exquisite creations. And thanks to my other generous supporters, my husband and daughters, for patiently tolerating my jewellery obsession.

Picture Credits
All images are Copyright © the designer named in the caption with the exception of the following:

1 In 2009 designer Marc Newson created a piece of high jewellery for Boucheron inspired by fractals — geometric shapes which incorporate smaller identical copies of the main shape in the pattern — using 2,000 sapphires and diamonds. Newson named it Julia, after Gaston Julia who, in the 1900s, discovered the mathematical formula on which the necklace was modelled.

2 Monica Bellucci for Cartier. Secrets et Merveilles collection. Necklace in platinum with 5 emerald-cut yellow diamonds, 1 kite-cut diamond (17.01 carats), 1 square-cut diamond, baguette-and-brilliant-cut diamonds. Photo: Vincent Peters © Cartier 2009.

6 Photo: Tiffany & Co.

9 Above: Cartier Archives. © Cartier.

10 Below left: N. Welsh, Cartier Collection. © Cartier. Below right: N. Welsh, Cartier Collection. © Cartier. Bottom left: N. Welsh, Cartier Collection. © Cartier.

11 Above: The Royal Collection © 2010, Her Majesty Queen Elizabeth II.

12 Christian Dior haute couture, spring/summer 2008. Photo: Chris Moore/Catwalking/Getty Images.

13 Top: Hakone (Japan), Lalique Museum. Photo courtesy Lalique.

14 Right: Private collection. Photo courtesy Lalique. Far right: Copyright © V&A Images/Victoria and Albert Museum. Below: Photo: Bob Thomas/Popperfoto/Getty Images.

15 Below left: Hakone (Japan), Lalique Museum. Photo courtesy Lalique. Below right: Photo courtesy Lalique.

16 Alexander McQueen, autumn/winter 2008/09. Photo: Karl Prouse/Catwalking/Getty Images.

17 Above: Photo: Jeffrey Mayer/WireImage.

18 Bottom right: Courtesy Frost of London.

19 Top left: Copyright © V&A Images/Victoria and Albert Museum.

20 Holly Fulton, London Fashion Week 2009. Photo: Karl Prouse/Catwalking/Getty Images.

21 Top left: Courtesy Peter Edwards. Top right: Photo: Nick Welsh, Cartier Collection © Cartier.

22 Below left: Courtesy Peter Edwards. Below right: Courtesy Sotheby's. Bottom right: Courtesy Sotheby's.

24 Photo: Thomas Schenk/Vogue © The Condé Nast Publications Ltd.

26 Top left: © Mikimoto Pearl Island Co. Ltd. Centre: © Mikimoto Pearl Island Co. Ltd.

27 Above: Photo: Tim Graham/Getty Images.

28 Alexander McQueen prêt-à-porter, autumn/winter 2009. Photo: Antonio de Moraes Barros Filho/WireImage.

29 Top right: Photo: Katel Riou © Cartier 2008. Above: Photo: Catwalking/Getty Images.

30 Above: Photo: Lipnitzki/Roger Viollet/Getty Images.

32 Photo: Emma Summerton/Vogue © The Condé Nast Publications Ltd.

34 Above: Courtesy Vedura. Bottom left: Courtesy Sotheby's. Below left: Courtesy Peter Edwards. Below right: Courtesy Sotheby's.

35 Above: Photo: Lipnitzki/Roger Viollet/Getty Images.

36 Viktor & Rolf for Swarovski. Courtesy Swarovski.

38 Above: Photo: Terence Donovan Archive/Getty Images.

39 Top left: Courtesy Peter Edwards. Above: Courtesy Sotheby's.

40 Erdem, spring/summer 2010. Photo: Chris Jackson/Getty Images.

42 Above: Photo: Carlton Davis. Top right: Photo: Tiffany & Co. Top left: Courtesy Sotheby's. Centre left: Courtesy Sotheby's. Centre right: Courtesy Sotheby's.

44 Above: Courtesy Sotheby's.

45 Photo: Mark Mattock/Vogue © The Condé Nast Publications Ltd.

46 Gareth Pugh, spring/summer 2009. Photo: Karl Prouse/Catwalking/Getty Images.

47 Centre: Courtesy Talisman Gallery. Above: Courtesy Shaun Leane.

48 Above: Courtesy Adrian Sassoon. Below left: Photo: David Watkins. Below centre: Photo: David Watkins. Below right: Photo: Keystone Features/Hulton Archive/Getty Images.

49 Top left: Photo: Steve Granitz/WireImage. Above: Photo: Michael Ochs Archives/Getty Images.

50 Photo: Eric Ryan/Getty Images.

51 Above: Photo: Venturelli/WireImage.

54 Calvin Klein, spring 2008. Photo: Biasion Studio/WireImage.

55 Top left: Photo: Josh Haskin. Above: Photo: Karl Prouse/Catwalking/Getty Images.

56 Top left: Photo © Denis Reggie 1996.

57 Top: Photo: Courtesy Georg Jensen. Above: Photo: Courtesy Georg Jensen. Below left: Photo: Courtesy Georg Jensen. Below right: Photo: Courtesy Georg Jensen.

58 From top: pearl and diamond drop earrings by David Morris; golden pearl strand by Harry Winston; three-row South sea pearl necklace by Graff; freshwater pearl strand by Theo Fennell; golden pearl strand by Mikimoto; diamond and pearl brooch by Tiffany. On arm: Perle et Ruban ring in 18-ct white gold, set with one South Sea pearl and 163 diamonds for a total weight of 1.35 ct by Chanel Fine Jewellery; pearl and diamond bracelet by Autore; diamond and pearl necklace worn underneath by Cartier; yellow gold and diamond bracelet by Bulgari; D-Flawless watch in 18 carat white gold, cultured pearls and diamonds by Chanel Fine Jewellery; pearl necklace by Belmacz. Photo: Ben Dunbar Brunton/Vogue © The Condé Nast Publications Ltd.

59 Above: Photo: Eric Feferberg/AFP/Getty Images.

60 Top centre: © Mikimoto Pearl Island Co. Ltd. Above: Photo: Time Life Pictures/Pictures Inc./Time Life Pictures/Getty Images.

61 Above: Photo: Art Rickerby/Time Life Pictures/Getty Images.

62 Louis Vuitton, spring/summer 2009. Photo: Chris Moore/Catwalking/Getty Images.

66 The Queen at Buckingham Palace wearing the Order of the Garter, 1953. Photo by Cecil Beaton. V&A Images/Victoria and Albert Museum, London.

67 Above: Photo: Venturelli/WireImage.

69 Above: Photo: Tim Graham/Getty Images.

70 Photo: David Montgomery/Vogue © The Condé Nast Publications Ltd.

71 Above: Photo: Randy Brooke/WireImage.

72 Below: Photo: Ron Galella/WireImage.

73 Above: Photo: Carola Polakov. Below left: Photo: Josh Haskin. Below right: Photo: Josh Haskin.

74 Dalí/Vogue/Condé Nast Archive; Copyright © Condé Nast.

75 Bottom: Photo: Venturelli/WireImage. Below: Photo: Courtesy Louisa Guinness.

76 Below: © Studio Lipnitzki/Roger-Viollet. Above: Photo: Jean-Jacques l'Héritier © Cartier. Below right: Photo: Nick Welsh, Cartier Collection © Cartier.

77 Top left: V&A Images/Victoria and Albert Museum, London. © Calder Foundation, New York/VG Bild-Kunst, Bonn, 2010. Top right: V&A Images/Victoria and Albert Museum, London. Reproduced by kind permission of Wendy Ramshaw.

78 Richard Nicoll, spring/summer 2009. Photo: Karl Prouse/Catwalking/Getty Images.

79 Above: Photo: Michael Thompson. Below: Photo: Tiffany & Co.

82 Diane von Furstenberg, spring/summer 2009. Photo: Chris Moore/Catwalking/Getty Images.

83 Top left and right: Photo: Nick Welsh, Cartier Collection © Cartier. Above: Photo: Antonio de Moraes Barros Filho/WireImage.

84 Above: Photo: Chris Jackson/Getty Images.

85 Top left: Courtesy Talisman Gallery. Centre left: Courtesy Talisman Gallery. Above: Courtesy Sotheby's.

86 Top left: Courtesy Harry Fane. Above: Courtesy Harry Fane.

87 The Maharani look by the Gem Palace. Photo: Calliope.

88 Cher at the 58th Annual Academy Awards, 1986. Photo: Jim Smeal/WireImage.

89 Above: Photo: RALSTON/AFP/Getty Images.

90 Above right: Courtesy Harry Winston. Above: Courtesy Harry Winston.

91 Above: Photo: Frank Edwards/Fotos International/Getty Images.

92 Photo: Edward Steichen/Vogue © The Condé Nast Publications Ltd.

93 Top left: Courtesy Peter Edwards. Top right: Courtesy Peter Edwards. Above: Photo: Karl Prouse/Catwalking/Getty Images.

94 Above: Photo: John Kobal Foundation/Getty Images. Top left: Courtesy Peter Edwards.

95 Above: Photo: Eugene Robert Richee/John Kobal Foundation/Getty Images. Below: Courtesy Peter Edwards. Bottom

left: Courtesy Sotheby's. Bottom right: Courtesy Sotheby's.

96 Tilda Swinton wears Pomellato's spring 2010 collection. Photo: Paolo Roversi.

98 Top left: Courtesy Peter Edwards. Above right: Photo: Tiffany & Co. Centre right: Photo: Tiffany & Co.

99 Above: Photo: Dave M. Benett/Getty Images.

100 Dior's New Look. Courtesy Christian Dior.

101 Below: Courtesy Sandra Cronan.

102 Top right: Courtesy Sotheby's. Top left: Courtesy Peter Edwards. Centre: Courtesy Peter Edwards. Above: Courtesy Sotheby's.

104 Photo: Thomas Schenk/Vogue © The Condé Nast Publications Ltd.

105 Above: Photo: Dave Benett/Getty Images.

106 Below: Photo: Karl Prouse/Catwalking/Getty Images.

108 Andre 3000 at the MTV Europe Music Awards 2004 in Italy. Photo: John Rogers/Getty Images.

109 Above: Photo: John Kobal Foundation/Getty Images. Centre right: Courtesy Sandra Cronan.

110 Above: Photo: Popperfoto/Getty Images. Below right: Cigarette case by Cartier. Bottom left: Photo: Gérard Panseri © Cartier 2009.

111 Top right: Photo: Nick Welsh, Cartier Collection © Cartier.

112 Christian Lacroix haute couture, autumn/winter 2009/10. Photo: Chris Moore/Catwalking/Getty Images.

113 Above: © Chanel.

114 Above: Photo: Rose Hartman/Getty Images.

116 Photo: Corinne Day/Vogue © The Condé Nast Publications Ltd.

119 Above: Photo: Matt Cardy/Getty Images. Bottom left: Courtesy Talisman Gallery.

120 Photo: Robert Erdmann/Vogue © The Condé Nast Publications Ltd.

121 Top centre: Courtesy Frost of London.

122 Above: © Popperfoto/Cosmos. Bottom: Photo: Nick Welsh, Cartier Collection © Cartier.

123 Above: Cartier Archives © Cartier.

124 Christopher Kane, London Fashion Week 2009. Photo: Heathcliff O'Mall/Catwalking/Getty Images.

130 Photo: Yamashiro/Vogue © The Condé Nast Publications Ltd.

134–5 Photos: Pascal Chevalier/Vogue © The Condé Nast Publications Ltd.

136 Carolina Herrera, spring 2009. Photo: Frazer Harrison/Getty Images for IMG.

137 Top right: Courtesy Sandra Cronan.

140 Photo: Willy Vanderperre/Vogue © The Condé Nast Publications Ltd.

142 Top right: Courtesy of Peter Edwards. Below: Photo: Kevin Mazur/WireImage.

143 Below left: Private collection. Image Courtesy of Wartski, London. Below right: V&A Images/Victoria and Albert Museum, London.

144 Jil Sander, autumn/winter 2009. Photo: Nathalie Lagneau/Catwalking/Getty Images.

145 Top: Photo: Nick Welsh, Cartier Collection © Cartier

147 Centre left: Photo: Tiffany & Co.

148 Photo: Courtesy Karl Lagerfeld.

149 Top left: Photo: Patrick Swirc. Below:

Photo: Vince Bucci/Getty Images.

152 Photo: Robert Erdmann/Vogue © The Condé Nast Publications Ltd.

153 Above: Photo: Karl Prouse/Catwalking/Getty Images.

154 Above: Photo: Robert Mora/WireImage.

155 Above: Photo: Matthew Rolston/Warner Bros./Getty Images. Below (cuff with silver): Courtesy Talisman Gallery.

156 Photo: Robert Erdmann/Vogue © The Condé Nast Publications Ltd.

160 Viktor & Rolf prêt-à-porter, spring/summer 2010. Photo: Karl Prouse/Catwalking/Getty Images.

161 Top right: Courtesy Talisman Gallery.

162 Above: Photo: Chris Moore/Catwalking/Getty Images. Below right: Courtesy Talisman Gallery.

163 Top left and right: Photo: Richard Pierce. Centre: Photo: David Sawyer. Above: Photo: Manuel Cohen/Getty Images. Photo of Frank Gehry: David Livingston/Getty Images.

164 Emilio Pucci, autumn 2008. Photo: Antonio de Moraes Barros Filho/FilmMagic.

168 Louis Vuitton prêt-à-porter, autumn/winter 2011. Photo: Dominique Charriau/WireImage.

169 Top left: Courtesy Sandra Cronan. Top right: Courtesy Sandra Cronan. Above: Private collection. Image courtesy of Wartski, London.

170 Above: Photo: Chris Moore/Catwalking/Getty Images. Below: Private collection. Image courtesy of Wartski, London. Bottom left: Private collection. Image courtesy of Wartski, London. Bottom right: Private collection. Image courtesy of Wartski, London.

171 Above: Photo: Alberto E. Rodriguez/Getty Images.

Front flap: Multicoloured pearls, sapphires and diamonds
Swing brooch by Chanel Fine Jewellery (see p. 61).
Front cover: Photo: Kai Z. Feng; fashion editor: Gillian
Wilkins; model: Eniko Mihalik at Storm Models.
Back cover: Top right: Christian Dior haute couture, spring/
summer 2008. Photo: Chris Moore/Catwalking/Getty
Images (see p. 12).
Bottom left: p. 20 Holly Fulton, London Fashion Week 2009.
Photo: Karl Prouse/Catwalking/Getty Images (see p. 20).
Bottom right: Wrapped heart brooch with rubies by Verdura
(see p. 35).
Back flap: White Light by Shaun Leane in collaboration
with Steinmetz for the Forevermark Precious collection
(see p. 99).

Prestel would like to thank

gettyimages®

for their kind cooperation

Prestel, a member of Verlagsgruppe Random House GmbH

Prestel Verlag
Königinstrasse 9
80539 Munich
Tel. +49 (0)89 24 29 08-300
Fax +49 (0)89 24 29 08-335

www.prestel.de

Prestel Publishing Ltd.
4 Bloomsbury Place
London WC1A 2QA
Tel. +44 (0)20 7323-5004
Fax +44 (0)20 7636-8004

Prestel Publishing
900 Broadway, Suite 603
New York, NY 10003
Tel. +1 (212) 995-2720
Fax +1 (212) 995-2733

www.prestel.com

Library of Congress Control Number: 2010927815

British Library Cataloguing-in-Publication Data: a catalogue
record for this book is available from the British Library;
Deutsche Nationalbibliothek holds a record of this publication
in the Deutsche Nationalbibliografie; detailed bibliographical
data can be found under: http://dnb.d-nb.de

Prestel books are available worldwide. Please contact
your nearest bookseller or one of the above addresses
for information concerning your local distributor.

Editorial direction: Philippa Hurd
Design, layout and typesetting: Praline, London
Production: Christine Groß
Origination: Reproline Mediateam, Munich
Printing and Binding: Appl, Wemding

FSC
Mix
Produktgruppe aus vorbildlich
bewirtschafteten Wäldern,
kontrollierten Herkünften und
Recyclingholz oder -fasern
Product group from well-managed
forests, controlled sources and
recycled wood or fibre
Zert.-Nr. SGS-COC-004238
www.fsc.org
© 1996 Forest Stewardship Council

Verlagsgruppe Random House FSC-DEU-0100
The FSC-certified paper Galaxi Brillant has been supplied
by Papier Union.

ISBN 3-7913-4484-3